# The MESOAMERICAN SOUTHWEST

Readings in Archaeology, Ethnohistory, and Ethnology

EDITED BY

**BASIL C. HEDRICK**

**J. CHARLES KELLEY**

**CARROLL L. RILEY**

*Southern Illinois University Press*    *Carbondale and Edwardsville*

*Feffer & Simons, Inc.*    *London and Amsterdam*

**Library of Congress Cataloging in Publication Data**

Hedrick, Basil Calvin, 1932–      comp.
   The Mesoamerican Southwest.

   Includes bibliographical references.
   1. Indians of North America—Southwest, New—Antiquities—Addresses, essays,
lectures.   2. Southwest, New—Antiquities—Addresses, essays, lectures.   3. Indians of Mexico—Antiquities—Addresses, essays, lectures.   4. Mexico—Antiquities
—Addresses, essays, lectures.
I. Kelley, J. Charles, 1913–      joint comp.   II. Riley, Carroll L., joint comp.
III. Title. E78.S7H44      970.4'9      74–10637      ISBN 0–8093–0665–4

*TO*
*ANNE*
*ELLEN*
*BRENT*

# CONTENTS

Preface               ix

**PART 1**

1   The Mesoamerican Southwest     3
*Basil C. Hedrick   J. Charles Kelley   Carroll L. Riley*

**PART 2**

Introduction     10

2   Guayule: A Rubber Plant of the Chihuahuan Desert    12
*Francis Ernest Lloyd*

3   A Prehistoric Rubber Ball    15
*Charles Amsden*

4   A Pre-Spanish Rubber Ball from Arizona    17
*Emil W. Haury*

**PART 3**

Introduction     24

5   The Ruins of Casas Grandes—I    25
*Adolph F. Bandelier*

6   The Ruins of Casas Grandes—II    31
*Adolph F. Bandelier*

**PART 4**

Introduction     38

7   The Discovery of New Mexico by Fray Marcos of Nizza    40
*Adolph F. Bandelier*

**PART 5**

Introduction      50

8    Cultural Relations between Northern Mexico and the
     Southwest United States: Ethnologically and
     Archaeologically      52
     *Ralph L. Beals*

9    Relations between Mesoamerica and the Southwest      58
     *Ralph L. Beals*

**PART 6**

Introduction      66

10    On the Pueblo IV and on the Kachina-Tlaloc Relations    68
     *J. O. Brew*

**PART 7**

Introduction      74

11    The Butterfly in Hopi Myth and Ritual      75
     *J. Walter Fewkes*

**PART 8**

Introduction      90

12    The Problem of Contacts between the Southwestern
     United States and Mexico      92
     *Emil W. Haury*

**PART 9**

Introduction      104

13    Native Culture of the Southwest      106
     *A. L. Kroeber*

**PART 10**

Introduction      128

14    Some Aztec and Pueblo Parallels      131
     *Elsie Clews Parsons*

Notes      149

Index      173

# PREFACE

In this volume, as in the two previous ones, we have standardized the various papers using, in this case, expanded footnotes and no bibliography. Minor corrections have been made and in some cases illustrative material has been eliminated. We have to some degree standardized spellings; for example in Brew's article we have changed the spelling of the word Katchina to Kachina in keeping with contemporary usage. In volume two (*The Classic Southwest*) we spoke of the "glorious inconsistency" of Bandelier in handling footnotes and references and decided to let them stand as that author presented them. In this volume, however, we have eliminated many of the citations, though not the descriptive footnotes. The nineteenth-century spellings of such names as Nizza (Niza) and Estevan or Estevanico (Esteban) have been maintained.

We acknowledge with gratitude the following people who have helped with this book: The fine editorial work of D. Kathleen Abbass and Judith W. Grimes represents a major contribution to the production of the volume. To Vicky Wuehler, Teresa Courson, Barbara Crump, Joan Prusacki, and Pat Radtke go our appreciation of their loyal service in manuscript preparation.

In instances where the authors of works reproduced here are living or where the works concerned are still protected by copyright we have obtained permission from the appropriate sources for publication in *The Mesoamerican Southwest*. Accordingly, special acknowledgment is made for permission to reprint the following works:

Ralph L. Beals for his articles "Cultural Relations between Northern Mexico and the Southwest United States: Ethnologically and Archaeologically" (title originally in Spanish), and "Relations between Mesoamerica and the Southwest." These originally appeared in the 1943 volume entitled: *El Norte de México y el sur de Estados Unidos, Tercera Reunión de Mesa Redonda sobre Problemas Antropológicos de México y Centro América*, 25 de Agosto a 2 de Septembre de 1943 (México, 1943), pp. 191–99, and pp. 245–52.

Appearing on pp. 241–45 of the same volume as the two Beals articles is that of J. O. Brew, entitled "On the Pueblo IV and on the Kachina-Tlaloc relations."

Emil W. Haury for permission to reprint two articles in this volume. They are: "A Pre-Spanish Rubber Ball from Arizona" from *American Antiquity* 2 (1937): 282–88, and "The Problem of Contacts Between the Southwestern United States and Mexico" is from the *Southwestern Journal of Anthropology* 1 (1945): 55–74.

"A Prehistoric Rubber Ball" by Charles Amsden was first published in *Masterkey* 10 (1936): 7–8.

"The Discovery of New Mexico by Fray Marcos of Nizza" by Adolph F. Bandelier appeared in *Magazine of Western History* 5 (1886): 659–70; it was reprinted in *New Mexico Historical Review* 4 (1929): 28–44, and appeared again in a condensed version in the *Masterkey* 2 (1929): 5–15. Bandelier's article "The Ruins of Casa Grandes" was published in two parts in the *Nation*, no. 1313 (1890), pp. 166–68 and no. 1314 (1890), pp. 185–87.

We express appreciation to the *American Anthropologist* for publication of the following articles: J. W. Fewkes, "The Butterfly in Hopi Myth and Ritual," *American Anthropologist* 12 (1910): 576–94; Elsie Clews Parsons, "Some Aztec and Pueblo Parallels," *American Anthropologist* 35 (1933): 611–31.

*Native Culture of the Southwest* by A. L. Kroeber is from the University of California Publications in American Archaeology and Ethnology 23 (1928): 375–98.

The book *Guayule: A Rubber-Plant of the Chihuahuan Desert* by Francis Ernest Lloyd was first published in 1911 by the Carnegie Institution of Washington, D.C. Pages 4–6 of that volume are reprinted here.

Basil C. Hedrick
J. Charles Kelley
Carroll L. Riley

*Carbondale, Illinois*
*October 1973*

*PART 1*

# THE MESOAMERICAN SOUTHWEST

## Basil C. Hedrick
## J. Charles Kelley
## Carroll L. Riley

In two previous volumes, *The North Mexican Frontier*[1] and *The Classic Southwest*,[2] we have brought together a series of papers—some long out of print—by important early investigators of the Greater Southwest. The articles by distinguished archaeologists, ethnographers, ethnohistorians, and other specialists reproduced in this third volume of readings have been selected with a view to focusing the attention of the reader on the impressive amount of evidence for an intimate relationship between the cultures of Mesoamerica and the American Southwest that had already been accumulated in various fields by the midpoint of this century. The earlier Southwestern scholars, who were often composite archaeologists, ethnographers, ethnohistorians, and geographers, in general accepted such relationships as obvious, and made little attempt therefore to examine critically the hypotheses involved. Subsequent scholars therefore, lacking firm archaeological evidence of the time depth for Mesoamerican elements in the Southwest, began to believe that these Mesoamerican elements might well have been introduced either by the early Spanish *conquistadores* or by the Mexican Indians who accompanied them on the first *entradas*. Concentration on detailed studies of Southwestern ceramics, architecture, and other traits, together with emphasis on the empirical evidence of typology and stratigraphy, accompanied later by the techniques of dendrochronology and ceramic technology, led many archaeologists to the firm conviction that the Southwestern cultural development was essentially indigenous and self-contained, aside from the early penetration into the area (presumably from Mexico) of cultigens and, later, of such "insignificant" items as copper bells. There arose what was essentially a cult of "card-carrying" Southwestern archaeologists firmly convinced that such an hypothesis provided ample explanation for the observed phenomena of Southwestern culture history.

Intensive archaeological work in the Hohokam culture area of the Southwest quickly cast doubt on this hypothesis. Newly discovered "ball courts," rubber balls, Mesoamerican-type composite mirrors, and conch shell trumpets, among other things, were difficult to dismiss as casual and insignificant introductions from Mesoamerica. Similar doubts began to grow among the ethnologists. By the early 1940s these doubts had begun to crystallize into a growing conviction among some archaeologists and ethnologists that the earlier scholars had, indeed, been correct and that the dependence of the Southwest on Mesoamerica might be much greater than was then currently believed. These views were effectively crystallized in the important papers by Beals, Brew, and Haury reproduced in this volume.

After a hiatus in fieldwork and, to some extent, in publication during and immediately following World War II, a new series of field studies began in archaeology and ethnography in both northwestern Mexico and the American Southwest. With this new work there came into being a new group of scholars who soon became convinced that the Southwestern cultural development must have been influenced by Mesoamerica to an extent even exceeding that visualized by the early Southwestern scholars. A paper by Edwin Ferdon,[3] produced an historic breakthrough for the new school of belief. Ferdon pointed out that even in the Chaco Canyon, the very citadel of Classic Anasazi development, there were strong evidences of Mesoamerican contact, which he tentatively attributed to the presence of refugee Toltec nobles, who had fled there following the demise of Tula! Following Ferdon, the Southwestern Seminar held in Santa Fe, New Mexico in 1955 concluded that the Southwest had been under intensive acculturation pressure from Mesoamerica throughout its existence as a separate cultural entity.[4]

During the following decade an impressive new series of studies in both the Southwest and Northwestern Mesoamerica pointed conclusively to the dependence of Southwestern cultural developments on influences from Mesoamerica. The excavation of the Gatlin site in Arizona,[5] for example, and the magnificent reexcavation of Snaketown by Haury clearly demonstrated the Mesoamerican origins of Hohokam culture. Continued work in northwestern Mexico identified and explained the sources of the Mesoamerican influences which had so strongly influenced the development of Southwestern culture. DiPeso's intensive excavations at Casas Grandes, in Chihuahua,[6] identified conclusively one of the peripheral Mesoamerican centers from which these influences penetrated the Southwest. The work of Schroeder[7] painstakingly defined the channels of diffusion of Mexican influences into the Southwest. It became clearly evident that during much of their history the various cultures of the American Southwest had developed along lines essentially determined by developments in Mesoamerica, but jointly conditioned by local ecology and traditions into a recognizably unique cultural sphere of their own.

The recent development of the "New Archaeology" in the Southwest channeled investigations and interpretations into a somewhat different conceptualization of Southwestern cultural history. Some of the "New Archaeologists" have chosen to interpret the aboriginal Southwest as essentially self contained—treating the cultural development and area as a closed system in which known or assumed influences from the outside are ignored. However, this approach *does* take into account and largely excludes from theoretical consideration the Spanish Conquest of the native Southwesterners and consequent changes in their culture. Otherwise, these investigators would be faced with the problem of explaining Spanish Catholicism among the Pueblos—and many other traits of Old World origin—as part of the evolution of Puebloan religion and ceremonialism! If indeed the "New Archaeologists" elect to exclude one known complex of extraneous influences from their consideration, then they logically should also exclude other known intrusions—specifically, massive Mesoamerican influences over a period of more than two millennia.

In terms of our present knowledge, exclusion of known Mesoamerican influences from considerations of the development and functioning of Southwestern society and culture would leave very little to work with. On the contrary, so many confirmatory data are now available that we must reasonably conclude that the older Southwestern archaeologists were essentially correct. It is now possible to demonstrate on both archaeological and ethnological grounds that throughout most of its history the Southwest was tied to Mesoamerica by elaborate routes of trade along which much of Mesoamerican culture was diffused northward. So complete was this dependence, that Southwestern cultural development must have more than once been strongly affected by major historical events in far-off central Mexico. When Teotihuacan dominated Mesoamerica, the trade routes northward seem to have followed principally the central route, up the eastern margins and foothills of the Sierra Madre Occidental into New Mexico and Arizona. After Teotihuacan fell, a new trade route was developed up the west coast of Mexico, and the traders who traversed it carried with them various complexes of Postclassic traits. The rise of a strong Tarascan empire in West Mexico in later Postclassic times seems to have temporarily closed this route. The Tarascans themselves thereafter began to reestablish this old west coast route, Tarascan traders replacing Aztec and Toltec predecessors. Shortly thereafter the Spanish Conquest took place and Mesoamerica and, somewhat later, the Southwest were subjected to major changes.

However, the vast changes that came to Mesoamerica as a result of Spanish intrusion, conquest, and settlement did not at first greatly alter trade and other relationships between the Southwest and northern Mexico and outside peoples. In the early sixteenth century both the Piman and Pueblo peoples were engaged in far flung trade in several directions. The late prehistoric levels of sites such as Pecos, on the very eastern fringes of the Southwest, show extensive trade in shells from the Gulf of Mexico and California and from the Pacific.[8] Parrot and macaw feathers and probably live birds continued to flow northward while turquoise and other semijewel stones, and most likely items such as buffalo hides, cotton blankets, and salt, were traded to the south. In 1536 the Vaca party, probably somewhere in the Sonora Valley, intercepted such a trade route, perhaps that of the Tarascans. As gifts from traders who were in contact with the Pueblo area—or possibly from Pueblo Indians, the context is unclear—Vaca and his companions received "emeralds shaped like arrowheads."[9] Three years later Fr. Marcos de Niza and Esteban de Dorantes, the black slave of the Vaca party, were sent north to explore the Southwest. Esteban, at least, reached Zuñi where local Indians recognized a shaman's rattle that he had obtained earlier, probably in northern Mexico.[10] At about the same time Marcos himself spoke with Pueblo Indians in the Gila-Salt area.[11] Pueblo Indians were also interviewed by Melchior Díaz a few months later somewhere in the Gila or Salt River valley.[12] Even more significant was the fact that Alarcón, in 1540, found Indians on the lower Colorado River who had visited Pueblo country (surely to trade) and who seemed to know the Pima area as well.[13]

In fact, the Coronado expedition of 1540 is in itself a tribute to a widespread knowledge of the Southwest. Guided over a well-known and well-traveled route, Coronado never failed to maintain linguistic contact with even the most remote peoples. It is obvious that his Pima or Opata guides either could speak Puebloan languages, or peoples as far apart as those of Zuñi and Pecos spoke Sonoran tongues. In addition, there are tantalizing suggestions that Nahuatl was used at least to some degree in Pueblo country.[14] Contacts between the Southwest and the Great Plains and beyond are also well documented by Coronado. The Spaniards were guided by two Plains Indians on a roundabout trip from Pecos to the Palo Duro Canyon area, then northeastward to Quivira in central Kansas. These guides, "The Turk" and Isopete, were slaves (whatever *that* might mean) at Pecos. "The Turk" especially had wide knowledge of peoples and places, for he told the Spaniards stories that seem to describe the contemporary Mississippian culture of the eastern United States.[15]

After Coronado left the Southwest, a number of stragglers from the expedition eventually worked their way back to New Spain. Two Indian "Donados" from the Tarascan country actually penetrated again to Quivira with the priest, Juan de Padilla. From there they trekked homeward, seemingly with no great difficulty; "home" beginning at Culiacan on the west coast of Mexico.[16]

Other Indians left behind by Coronado undoubtedly somewhat reinforced the strong Mexican flavor of the Southwest. But much of that flavor, especially in religion, was already centuries old. The masked dances, sophisticated development of sky and earth deities, divine twins, deeply integrated association of colors and directions, organized priesthoods who controlled curing, weather, individual and group welfare, and exercised powerful sanctions—both divine and secular—against malefactors; all point to a Mesoamerican homeland.[17] So do the extensive symbolism and various specific material traits found in the archaeological record. Peyote, known to have been used in early Spanish New Mexico, may also point to long contact with the interior of Mexico.

Active Mesoamericanization of the Southwest, however, had come to an end by the last years of the sixteenth century. The early Spanish expeditions had aided it a bit by introducing more Mesoamerican Indians, but they also brought alien ideas and peoples. Blacks came from the Coronado and later expeditions and some remained in the Southwest from Coronado's time. These individuals surely introduced a mixture of Spanish and African customs.[18] Most importantly, however, were the cultural blows struck at the Mesoamerican homeland. By 1530 the Mesoamerican Great Tradition had been destroyed in its central Mexican heartland. Probably the Pochteca organizations that penetrated the Southwest were not entirely dependent on the elaborate Aztec and Tarascan political organizations. Therefore, they likely survived the collapse of the central Mexican kingdoms, especially if trade and other associated contacts tended to radiate out from regional centers. Even so, the effect of material and spiritual destruction of the Aztec and Tarascan cultures must have been very harsh, and a more telling blow was soon to come. By the mid-sixteenth century sub-Mexican cultures to the east and west of Mexica-Tarasco had crumbled. The west coast never recovered from the depredations of Guzmán, and the Pánuco region to the east stagnated under Spanish misrule. By 1580 Spanish mining colonies were in southern Chihuahua, only a few hundred miles from the southern-most Pueblo settlements. The period 1581 to 1598 saw no less than six major incursions into Pueblo territory, and the sixth (that of Oñate) came to stay.

Their ties with Mesoamerican culture cut off and, facing stringent forced acculturation by Spanish priests and soldiers, the Pueblo Indians clung tenaciously to the cultural and religious synthesis worked out over the centuries. Central Mexican traders working on an individual or family basis continued to penetrate the Southwest into the nineteenth century,[19] but their cultural wares were now mainly Spanish and their religion, at least formally, was Christian. Pima and Papago Indians to the south had a respite for a century as Spanish routes shifted east of the Sierra Madre but by 1700 they, too, faced forced missionization. That same period saw the last desperate attempt of the Pueblo Indians to throw off Spanish rule and Spanish influence. After the reconquest of Pueblo land (ca. 1700), there was—curiously—a somewhat reduced pressure to destroy "Indian" ways but Spanish (and later, American) elements continued to be gradually added to the cultural stock of Southwestern Indians. Still and all the synthesis remained basically a Southwestern variant of Meso-american religion and culture as, indeed, it is today.

---

PART 2

# INTRODUCTION

One of the most dramatic indications of contacts between Meso-america and the upper Southwest is that of the Mesoamerican-type ritual ball game. This game, known from Postclassic Mexico and the Maya area, has been well described in early Spanish sources. It was played on a rectangular, usually masonry court, using a rubber ball. The actual style of the court varied from time to time and from place to place and, presumably, the rules of the game may also have varied. However, the game was intimately associated with religious ceremonies and an ubiquitous feature was the rule that the heavy rubber ball not be struck with the hands. Ball courts of a rather typical late Mesoamerican type laid out in the form of an "I" have been noted from as far north as Casas Grandes in Chihuahua.[1]

During the last two decades, other evidence has accumulated from diverse sources suggesting the diffusion through the peripheral Mesoamerican cultures of northwestern Mexico of an earlier and smaller type of ball court which may yet be identified in the South-west. Thus, in 1956 at the Schroeder site near the city of Durango, a small ball court of very simple form was excavated. This court, oriented north-south, had an open-ended playing alley some four meters in width and ten meters in length. The playing alley itself was enclosed on the east and west only by two narrow parallel stone masonry platforms, apparently representing a low terrace or bench along each side and a higher terrace or bench above this, in both cases with outward slanting walls. The court was probably built during the Ayala phase of the Chalchihuites culture ca. A.D. 550–700. In the summer of 1972 an almost identical court, as yet unex-cavated, was found at the site of Gualterio Abajo some sixty miles southeast of the Schroeder site. The cultural context suggests a dat-ing at ca. A.D. 100–300. Interestingly enough, several ceramic models of almost identical courts, in terms of both size and form, with players actually engaged in the game—usually three on each side—have turned up in collections which almost certainly origi-nated in the shaft tomb culture in Nayarit-Jalisco. The culture in question is tentatively dated ca. 200 B.C. to A.D. 500, bringing the ceramic ball court models in line with the dating of those found further north. Curiously enough in view of the small size of the rubber balls described in the papers reproduced here, the Nayarit-Jalisco balls are depicted as basketball size or larger.

The ball game itself, although not played on a prepared court, but with the same basic rules for handling the ball, has been cited ethnographically for various West Mexican peoples as far north as the Cáhita area.[2] In the 1930s, the excavations at the great Hohokam site of Snaketown, near Phoenix, brought to light what seems to be a crude, though sizeable Mesoamerican ball court and, since that date, a number of other courts have been described in the Hohokam area.[3] The identification of the courts has, indeed, been challenged and some of them may, in fact, be dance platforms.[4] It is still generally accepted, however, that the large Snaketown-type of court was, indeed used for the ball game.[5]

One of the interesting things about the ball game in Mesoamerica is that, although there are historic references to the type of ball used, such balls are very rare in the archaeological records if, indeed, they exist at all. Interestingly, three rubber balls, uncovered early in the twentieth century, have been reported from southern Arizona. Although none of these three were discovered as a result of controlled excavations, there seems little reason to doubt that they are, in fact, pre-Columbian. Two of the balls came to light around 1909, at a dam site at the west end of the Santa Cruz Reservoir in association with prehistoric remains. One was examined by a Professor R. H. Forbes, but no determination was made as to the type of rubber from which it was made. This rubber ball seems subsequently to have been lost, but the second one from the same area later was given to the Southwest Museum and is probably made from the guayule plant (*Parthenium argentatum* Gray) which grows in parts of the interior plateaus of Mexico and in Texas. A third rubber ball was found in the early days near Casa Grande but seems to have disappeared without a trace.

The articles by Lloyd, Amsden, and Haury reproduced below give much of the basic data on these unique occurrences and represent part of the evidence for this particular Mesoamerican complex. Taken alone, the occurrences might be explained in terms of kickball or some other non-Mesoamerican game. In conjunction with the courts and with the many other Mesoamerican traits now clearly demonstrated as appearing in the pre-Columbian Southwest,[6] the rubber balls take on a certain importance as collaborative evidence for these most important Mesoamerican-Southwestern contacts. The small size of the balls found, however, suggests an alternative usage for them: perhaps they represent a copal-like incense, to be burned in braziers at ceremonials! Such an alternative explanation, however, would only emphasize further the Mesoamerican origins of both the rubber balls and their function.

# GUAYULE: A RUBBER PLANT
# OF THE CHIHUAHUAN DESERT

**Francis Ernest Lloyd**

## The Vulgar Name

The name[1] "guayule" is properly applied only to *Parthenium argentatum* Gray. On account, however, of a superficial resemblance it has to certain other plants, especially because of similarities in size and in the gray color (so often seen in the desert) of the foliage, these have been wrongly called by the same name.[2] The mariola (*P. incanum* H. B. K.), a closely related species, is one of these; and its very general association with the guayule proper has led to much error in estimating acreage of guayule. It is of interest in this connection to note that the mariola is known to the peon, in some parts at any rate, as "hembra de guayule,"[3] apparently because of the very constant association of the two species, and because of the belief that this association is in some way necessary to the production of seed. Other species of the genus, some of which are annuals, have also received the name guayule, while a plant of the Sonoran Desert (Sonora and southern Arizona), *Encelia farinosa*, is not only mistaken today for guayule but is believed by many to contain rubber. The amount, if present at all, is so insignificant that it would certainly not repay consideration from a commercial point of view.

The guayule is known also as "yerba de hule" in the region of Pasaje, Durango, and simply as "hule" in some parts of Zacatecas and of Chihuahua. An alternative spelling "yule" (which occurs incorrectly as "llule" in "guallule") is used in some parts of San Luis Potosí. The name xihuite[4] occurs in northern Zacatecas and "about Saltillo"; copallin and afinador are other less-used designations. But the name "guayule" thus spelled is in the ascendant and will in all probability replace other names. Its derivation, in common with other Mexicanisms, has speculative interest. Seler[5] would refer it to *quahu* (wood, tree, or forest) and *olli* (rubber, Sp. *hule*), evidently believing it to be of Aztec origin. This etymology finds support in the aboriginal term *ulequahuitl*, said by Sahagún (1529) and Augustín Torquemada (1615) to be applied to a latex tree (probably *Castilloa*) producing *ulli*, a dark resin which becomes very elastic (Jumelie 1903). By inversion, we have *quahu + ule*. The suggestion that the derivation is from the Castilian *hay* (there is) and the Aztec *olli*, from which we therefore have *hayolli*, which becomes hayule and so guayule, can not be seriously entertained.

## Primitive and Later Uses

Contact with the country peon of Mexico reveals a great deal of resourcefulness in the use of many plants. In out of the way places a game is played with a small, very resilient ball, not purchased in the market. It proves on examination to be of very pure rubber, obtained by communal mastication of the bark of the guayule. Altamirano (1906) tells us that country boys obtain rubber in a similar manner also from tatanini," a name applied, in Querétaro, to *Parthenium incanum* and to *P. lyratum*. This custom dates back with fair certainty to the middle of the eighteenth century, having been noted by a Jesuit, one Negrete.[6]

Mr. W. H. Stayton, formerly captain in the U.S. Navy, when on duty in the Gulf of California, observed the Yaqui Indians ashore playing a game with a ball about twice the diameter of a baseball. The game consisted in throwing the ball from hip to hip. It is not unlikely that the ball was made of guayule rubber, which could have been obtained from the country east of the Sierra Madre, or even of rubber from tataniní, mariola, or other plant. The possibility that it came from the South is, however, not excluded. Peter Martyr (1569; published in 1830), Sahagún (1529), and Herrera (1492–1526) all speak of balls made of rubber made from latex trees.[7]

There can therefore be little doubt that, in common with the manufacture of mescal, extraction of fibers, and like primitive industries, the making of rubber balls from the guayule, just as from latex plants, antedates the invasion of Mexico by the Spaniard. It may be mentioned in passing that the method of extracting the rubber as above noted is analogous to the only widely used modern method of obtaining the crude rubber on a large scale, namely, by a purely mechanical process. The rationale of this will be seen beyond. In this connection a recent discovery of a piece of rubber which is undoubtedly of ancient origin on an old aboriginal village site in Arizona is of peculiar interest. Of this discovery the following account is furnished me by Prof. R. H. Forbes:

> The lump of rubber, a portion of which I recently handed you, was found in December (or thereabouts), 1909 at the west end of the

Santa Cruz Reservoir and Land Company's dam, 14 miles west of Sasco, Ariz. Mr. C. O. Austin, who was present, states that this ball of rubber was contained in a small olla with articles of stone belonging to the *older* prehistoric ruins of this country. The find was made at about 3 feet below the general surface which was formed by the off-wash of an adjacent low mountain. No traces of houses on the present level of the land, according to Mr. Austin, were visible. One other ball of rubber was found here, and is now in Col. W. C. Greene's collection at Cananea. I regard this find as genuine, as Mr. Austin is familiar with Salt River Valley ruins and his statements are confirmed by others.

Microscopic examination of the specimen to which Professor Forbes refers throws doubt on the view that it is guayule rubber, but a final statement can not at present be made.

A record of this kind would be incomplete without reference to the use of guayule as a fuel. On account of its resin content, the plant burns with a fierce, smoky flame, after the fashion of "fat pine"; so that whenever it was available it was invariably used as a fuel for the crude Mexican adobe smelters, ruins of which are frequently seen in the mining districts. In this way thousands of acres have been depleted of their guayule, a wasteful process which was quickly stopped when the value of the plant became known. It can scarcely be doubted that many peculiarities of local distribution within restricted regions are due to the pulling of the guayule for fuel. Thus a large smelter and a number of roasting furnaces were in operation at Cedros,[8] the head fraction of the hacienda of that name lying to the west of Mazapil, for a term of years, and this circumstance is often referred to by the peons to explain the absence of guayule in places where it would naturally be expected. The case is analogous to the use of walnut for fuel and fence rails in the early days in the eastern United States.

# A PREHISTORIC RUBBER BALL

## Charles Amsden

Recent investigations have established beyond reasonable doubt that some of the ancient inhabitants of Arizona played a game of ball in ball courts or small stadiums much like those used by the Maya of Mexico in early historic times. First of the courts to be identified definitely as such was at Snaketown, a village of the Hohokam people not far from the better-known ruin of Casa Grande, which likewise had its ball court. With Snaketown for a clue, another court was recently brought to light much farther north, near the modern city of Flagstaff. Archeologists familiar with the low mounds and shallow pits which are all that remain of most Hohokam towns now realize that the ball courts of Arizona will one day be numbered by the dozen. But this will hardly hold true for the balls, numerous though they must once have been.

The Maya used a solid rubber ball larger than a baseball, according to early Spanish records, but so far as known, none remains in existence. What the Arizonans used might easily have remained a mystery forever, since balls are small and perishable objects. But it happens that in 1924 Mrs. C. E. Wiswall gave Southwest Museum a collection of archeological objects from southern Arizona and northern Mexico. Dr. Emil W. Haury, assistant director of Gila Pueblo at Globe, Arizona, in looking over the catalogue of the collection recently, noticed an item of promise: "lump of rubber, possibly a ball." At once the object was brought forth and examined, and found to be a rounded, flattish lump the size of a small man's fist. The outside resembles dried clay, but underneath this crust is a hard black substance answering in every point the description of well-dried rubber. That it is such has just been determined by a chemist engaged by Gila Pueblo to analyze the object. He finds it "a natural, un-refined, and unvulcanized rubber hydrocarbon containing resins, waxes, and organic soluble materials in proportions similar to rubber contained in rubber-bearing plants of North America. The exact botanical source of the rubber cannot be determined without a more exhaustive research, both of the sample submitted and of the rubber-bearing plants, particularly those of southern United States and Mexico."

This smashed and hardened ball was dug from a Hohokam ruin not far from Casa Grande, but the exact circumstances of its finding were not recorded by the amateur archeologist who did the digging. Whether it was a "lost ball" or one carefully treasured matters little. Evidently it is a game ball, and as such it adds to our knowledge of what happened on the earth-banked sunken ball courts of Arizona a thousand years ago. And of course it raises other problems, as new finds in archeology always do. Was it traded in from Mexico, or did its users know the secret of extracting rubber from some local shrub? Every effort will be made to find a rubber expert who can give the answer.

# A PRE-SPANISH RUBBER BALL FROM ARIZONA[1]

## Emil W. Haury[2]

In the winter of 1934–35, a ball court, analogous in many details with those of Central America, was discovered at Snaketown on the Gila River Indian Reservation in south-central Arizona, during excavations conducted by Gila Pueblo. The announcement of a ball court 1500 miles from its supposed origin,[3] and in a region where it was entirely unexpected, met with skepticism until the discovery was verified by men qualified to judge from first hand knowledge acquired in the Middle American field. A new angle to the problem of relationships of Southwestern, Mexican, and Central American cultures was thus brought to the fore. Now, to add to this discovery, comes another find in the form of a rubber ball. It, too, was found in south-central Arizona and many, indeed, have been used in the game for which the courts were built. As in the case of the ball courts, the announcement of a ball made of rubber, antedating the Conquest, may arouse incredulity, but I record the facts here for the interested reader, firm in the opinion that the specimen is authentic.

For the actual finding of this ball, we must go back some twenty-seven years to the fall of 1909. Col. W. C. Greene, cattleman, was then constructing a long earthern dam to impound the flood water of the Santa Cruz River at a point a few miles south of Toltec, Arizona. As dirt was being moved from the west bank of the stream by means of scrapers, objects of Indian manufacture were turned up from what appeared to be an old village site. Among these was a jar containing a lump recognized as rubber by the workmen. Lloyd, in his treatise on guayule, quotes Prof. R. H. Forbes concerning this specimen.[4]

> The lump of rubber, a portion of which I recently handed you, was found in December (or thereabouts), 1909, at the west end of the Santa Cruz Reservoir and Land Company's dam. . . . Mr. C. O. Austin, who was present, states that this ball of rubber was contained in a small olla with articles of stone belonging to the older prehistoric ruins of this country. The find was made at about 3 feet below the general surface which was formed by the off-wash of an adjacent low mountain. No

traces of houses on the present level of the land,[5] according to Mr. Austin, were visible. One other ball of rubber was found here, and is now in Col. W. C. Greene's collection at Cananea. I regard this find as genuine, as Mr. Austin is familiar with Salt River Valley ruins and his statements are confirmed by others.

The "other ball" mentioned is the specimen with which this article deals. It remained in the Greene collection until 1924, when it was presented to the Southwest Museum. There it lay until September 1935, when Mr. Charles Amsden of the museum's staff and the writer chanced upon it while seeking other items of Hohokam origin. The potential value of this ball, if authentic, became especially apparent, in view of the fresh discovery of ball courts, as it would assist in confirming the function of the ball courts as well as in showing that the Indians of this region were familiar with rubber. My request for the loan of the specimen, so that a qualitative analysis of the rubber could be made, was granted without hesitation, a courtesy for which I am indebted to the Southwest Museum. Although we do not know exactly how the ball was found, none of the circumstances surrounding its discovery tend to throw doubt on its genuineness. However, an analysis seemed the best means of authenticating it; and, as will presently be shown, the analysis yielded nothing but confirmatory evidence.

A casual inspection would not enable one to identify the ball as anything but an uninteresting stone. Distorted out of round, probably by earth pressure, it has a maximum diameter of 86 mm. and a minimum diameter of 53 mm. Its present weight is seven ounces. The surface color varies from light to dark brown. This is partly due to an incrustation of lime, a patina possessed by most objects recovered from ruins in southern Arizona. While this is not a conclusive proof, it bears out the claim for antiquity. Oxidation of the rubber accounts further for the brownish color of the specimen. This process has formed a hard outer crust about 5 mm. in thickness which is finely seamed with cracks exposing a dark substance below. These cracks are largely the result of handling the specimen and squeezing it to test resilience. Surface contours, in general, are rough, probably caused by contact with hard particles in the soil. The blackish material beneath the crusted surface layer is rubber only partially oxidized, which still retains a surprising degree of elasticity. To test this material, the services of a rubber chemist were enlisted. Mr. C. A. Neville of the Product Control Division of the Samson Plant, U.S. Rubber Company, Los Angeles, California, kindly offered to undertake the examination, a cooperative gesture which is deeply appreciated. Results of the analysis, made by Mr. J. K. Fleshman, follow:

**DETAILS**

> Extractable Waxes and Resins ..................... 17.7%
>   (Acetone and Chloroform Extracts)
>
> Rubber Hydrocarbon ........................... 42.5%
>   (Chloroform Extract and Bromine Equivalent)
>
> Ash ......................................... .9%
>
> Organic Insoluble ............................ 38.9%
>   (Insoluble Oxides, Natural Plant Products, etc.)
>
> Sulfur ...................................... Trace
>
> 100.0%

**ANALYSIS DETAILS**

1. Physical Appearance:
   Dark brown, odorless, tacky material with low tensile strength but quite elastic.

2. Acetone Extract (Extracted 16 hrs.):
   (a) Acetone containing extract was colorless while hot.
   (b) A very small amount of white material settled out of solution while hot and stuck to bottom of flask
   (c) A white, waxy material precipitated from the cold solution.
   (d) Evaporation of acetone left a transparent, waxy material which had a sweet aromatic odor. Total extract—14.40%.

3. Total Sulfur (Slight trace).

4. Ash:
   (a) Upon heating, the substance melted to a thick, dark mass, and gave off an odor characteristic of burning rubber.
   (b) Total ash was 0.88%. Analysis of ash showed calcium, aluminum, iron, and magnesium present.

**REMARKS**

A rubber or rubberlike material.

(a) Contained no pitch or similar substance.
(b) Characteristic of sugars in natural rubber.

(c) Natural waxes or paraffin.

(d) Extract too great for Hevea rubber and too soft for Borneo origin; odor and appearance characteristic of extracts from North American rubber-bearing plants, although quantity less than would be expected.

If rubber, it is not vulcanized; factice also eliminated.

(a) Rubber present.

(b) Calcium probably from soil in which material was imbedded. Magnesuim characteristic of natural rubber.

5. Chloroform Extract:
   (a) Acetone extracted material extracted for four hours with chloroform. Solution remained clear. The extract was brown in color and had appearance of rubber. Total extract—24.2%.

   (a) Characteristic natural rubber extract.

   (b) Dissolved extract in totuol. 3.3% remained insoluble. Insoluble material was white, crystalline, and hard.

   (b) Material dissolved in totuol apparently rubber. Insoluble material natural resins and waxes not soluble in acetone.

   (c) Material dissolved in totuol reprecipitated with alcohol. 29.9%.

   (c) Further confirmation of rubber.

6. Treatment of Chloroform Extracted Residue:
   (a) The residue had lost all tackiness and stretch, yet still had appearance of containing some rubber. Burning still gave characteristic appearance and odor of rubber.

   (a) It is highly probable that the great age of the sample had caused oxidation of resins, waxes and rubber to products insoluble in either acetone or chloroform. These insoluble materials may also have occluded some of the rubber so that the established 4 hours was insufficient time to extract completely all rubber.

   (b) The residue was treated with bromine to obtain an estimate of the rubber hydrocarbon. The estimate was made on the rubber tetrabromide precipitated in alcohol. 21.6% rubber obtained.

   The remainder of the residue was acted on by the bromine to form insoluble materials. Whereas rubber tetrabromide is soluble in $CCl_4$, it was assumed that all tetrabromide dissolved by the $CCl_4$ and precipitated by alcohol was rubber tetrabromide and that the remainder was organic insoluble material.

**CONCLUSIONS**

The sample is a natural, unrefined, and unvulcanized rubber hydrocarbon containing resins, waxes, and organic insoluble materials in proportions similar to rubber obtained from rubber-bearing plants of North America. The exact botanical source of the rubber cannot be determined without a more exhaustive research, both of the sample submitted and of the rubber-bearing plants, particularly those of the southern United States and Mexico.

PRODUCT CONTROL DIVISION

U.S. Rubber Company—Samson Plant

C. A. Neville; per: J. K. Fleshman

The report leaves no doubt regarding the nature of the material of which the ball was made and its general origin, but the specific source remains undetermined. Chemists were hesitant to undertake further work on this point because of the uncertain factors involved, such as the contamination of the rubber by the natives in its preparation,[6] which might lead to negative results. However, the problem has been stated by Dr. H. I. Cramer, assistant professor of chemistry, University of Akron, who responded freely to many inquiries. Referring to the analysis made by Mr. Fleshman, Dr. Cramer writes:

> It will be seen that the acetone extractable material and other resinous products are usually high, and the rubber hydrocarbon content correspondingly low. These facts may be explained: (1) by assuming that the sample was originally Guayule rubber which . . . is indigenous to Mexico and southern United States; (2) that the sample was derived originally from high grade rubbers such as Castilloa, which is indigenous to Central America and northern South America, or from *Hevea Braziliensis*, indigenous to the Amazon district, and has in the course of years undergone extensive oxidation.[7]

In the absence of specific data we must resort to speculation regarding the origin. Because of the great distance involved, South America may be eliminated as a source of rubber. Similarly, a Central American source, although plausible, seems unlikely. From the distribution of the main rubber-bearing plants, guayule would seem to be the most likely source. The properties of this plant have been known for a long time to the residents of the region where it grows, and it is not assuming too much to say that this knowledge extended well into antiquity. Certain physical qualities of the rubber in the ball suggested a guayule origin to Dr. Cramer, but without further analysis this, naturally, cannot be regarded as final.

Archaeologically, the rubber ball from the Santa Cruz site is unique. Of the thousands of rubber balls that must have been in use in Mexico[8] and Central America, no actual specimens seem to have survived. For northern Mexico, likewise, none have been documented; but for the Southwest, in addition to the example described here, Mr. Frank Pinkley, superintendent of Southwestern Monuments, has informed the writer that a rubber ball was found years ago near Casa Grande National Monument. Unfortunately, this ball has disappeared.

An appraisal of the cultural background of the ball rests on the associated material from the same site which reached the Southwest Museum in 1924. In a catalogue supplied with the collection, the ball and the objects were given the same origin. The artifacts, mainly pottery and shell, are identifiable as the products of the Hohokam culture. The nature of the pottery permits its allocation specifically to the Sedentary period which may be roughly dated at A.D. 900–1200. Thus, we are entitled to state that the ball dates from pre-Spanish times, and that its age, in round numbers, may be placed at a thousand years. Although recent discoveries indicate that ball courts antedate this period in the Southwest, we also know that they lasted through the Sedentary period into the Classic period (A.D. 1200–1400). This makes it possible to synchronize the age of the ball and the use of the courts, a necessary point in substantiating the assertion that the ball may have been used in the game played in the courts, as was the practice in Central America.

The archaeological significance of the ball is lessened somewhat by our ignorance of the exact source of the rubber. Although we do not ordinarily think of it as a domestic product, guayule rubber was available to the Hohokam either by trade or expeditions to the Chihuahua desert, the nearest source. The fact that rubber balls were common to southern Arizona, Mexico, and Central America, along with ball courts, is in itself most significant. It argues strongly for a cultural connection of the several areas, the exact nature of which remains to be determined.

It is an interesting coincidence that, although this rubber ball was found twenty-seven years ago, and ball courts might have been identified seventeen years ago, following suggestions made by Pinkley after his cursory excavations at Casa Grande, positive identifications of these two probably complementary traits were not made until 1935.

# PART 3

# INTRODUCTION

In the spring of 1884 Adolph Bandelier made a long trip on horseback through the northern Sierra Madres. Starting at Fort Huachuca in Arizona, he rode southward to below Arizpe in the Sonora Valley, then turned eastward into Yaqui drainage and so finally across the mountains to Casas Grandes. After several weeks of investigating ruins in this area Bandelier, still on horseback, returned to the United States. The results of this trip are recorded in two articles in the *Nation* (1890) which appear here. Further data is given in the *Final Report*.[1] The day by day journals of the 1884 trip have also been published[2] and one of the sketches made at Casas Grandes is reproduced by Burrus.[3]

In the rather detailed descriptions of Casas Grandes reproduced in this volume, Bandelier draws freely on his own considerable knowledge of Southwestern archaeology and ethnology for comparative purposes. The historical materials on Casas Grandes were, in fact, collected in the period 1886–89 when Bandelier was doing extensive archival work in Mexico and in the Southwest.[4] At the time he wrote, Bandelier was justified in placing the Spanish discovery of Casas Grandes as seventeenth century, for the Obregón journal[5] which presents evidence that Ibarra's party reached the ruin in the 1560s, had not yet been recovered.

In his reconstruction of Casas Grandes society Bandelier was greatly influenced by Lewis H. Morgan and, like Morgan, rejected the idea that American Indians could have had a true class-structured society.[6] Recent work by DiPeso[7] at Casas Grandes, however, confirms the essentially urban and sophisticated nature—at least in certain periods—of Casas Grandes culture.

# 5

# THE RUINS OF CASAS GRANDES—I

## Adolph F. Bandelier

The name of Casas Grandes, or "Great Houses," has been applied for over two centuries to a group of fairly preserved Indian ruins in the canton of Galeana, state of Chihuahua, Mexico. These ruins are situated nearly due south of Deming, on the Southern Pacific Railroad, at a distance of one hundred miles from the United States boundary line. They lie within half a mile of the village of Casas Grandes, a thriftless agglomeration of decaying adobe houses inhabited by about twelve hundred people.

It is well to discriminate between the Casas Grandes of Chihuahua and the Casa Grande of Arizona, on the middle course of the Gila River, eighty-five miles northwest of Tucson. The latter means "Great House," because the only well-preserved ruin is a clumsy building, three stories of which still remain. At Casas Grandes none of the edifices are as intact as the one on the Gila, but the pueblo was more extensive, and in one instance four stories can be clearly discerned. The architecture of both places bears the same characteristics. They seem to have been reared by tribes occupying the same level of culture, having the same ideas of life, social organization, religion, and art. Of the Casa Grande it is positively known that the ancestors of the Pima Indians built and occupied it. Concerning the Casas Grandes no definite tradition is known. What was told me by an Opata Indian from Huachinera in the Sierra Madre, namely, that the Opatas built and held the pueblo, calling it Hue-hueri Kita (Great Houses), is not impossible, but far from certain, as yet.

The valley of Casas Grandes is one of the few fertile spots in northwestern Chihuahua, outside of the Sierra Madre. The little river affords permanent water for irrigation. Groves of tall cottonwood trees line its sandy banks. The soil is white and seems sterile. Nothing but low mezquite, ocotilla, cats-claws, and tasajo—all thorny shrubs—cover it with a dusty vegetation. But, wherever irrigated, this apparently arid ground is productive of rich yields. The climate is warm in summer. Snow not seldom falls in winter, for the altitude reaches four thousand feet, and the latitude is slightly less than 30°30'. High parching winds are felt along the whole valley more or less; at Corralitos and Janos more so than at Casas Grandes proper.

The main ruins cannot be separated, archaeologically or geographically, from the remainder of the banks of the stream from its formation at San Diego to Ascension, full eighty miles below. There are, however, two breaks in the extent of fertile bottoms. One is between Corralitos and Janos; the other between Janos and Ascension. These intervals are due to abrupt and arid heights or chains of heights, outposts of the Sierra Madre, through which the stream has forced a passage. There no extensive ruins can be looked for, whereas around Ascension (beginning at the north), Janos, and from Corralitos to a point above Casas Grandes, the remains of ancient habitations are frequent. They all bear the same general character. The material is a marly clay, and they indicate houses of one or more stories, usually in groups indicating small villages, the center of each group being occupied by a building apparently higher than the rest. The edifices are not contiguous, and the distances separating them vary a good deal. Large structures, also isolated from all the others, are not infrequent. This is chiefly the case at Ascension and along the rivers Palanganas and Piedras Verdes, by the junction of which at San Diego the Rio des Casas Grandes is formed. For miles away the mounds are seen to rise above the dusty levels. Excavations reveal walls of several feet in thickness, rooms completely filled with the pulverized material of which the upper stories and the roofs were made. Pottery, handsomely painted and with a thin, fine gloss, is frequently found entire, for, as no rocks were used in the construction of the houses, the fine rubbish has enveloped the fragile earthenware and protected instead of shattering it. Not infrequently the houses rest on terraces supporting the vestiges of parapets of clay.

The number of these groups of buildings is considerable. Between Casas Grandes and Corralitos, a distance of twenty-eight miles, I counted and surveyed not less than ten distinct clusters, not including the main ruins at the former place. It seems that the four vales or basins, so eminently fitted for the wants of an agricultural Indian stock, were inhabited by several branches of a tribe in the same manner as the Queres now inhabit the Rio Grande valley from Cochiti to San Felipe and the banks of the Jemez stream from Zia to Santa Ana, and the Tehuas the Rio Grande above San Ildefonso in three pueblos within a space of twelve miles. In times previous to the occupation of New Mexico by the Spaniards the pueblos were smaller, on an average, than they are now, but more numerous. From three hundred actual surveys made by me of as many pueblo ruins, I gather that the average number of souls did not exceed three hundred. There were of course some pueblos which, like Pecos, the Pueblo Bonito, and others, sheltered a much larger number, but they were exceptions. The rule was a number of small villages not far apart from each other. So the Piros occupied on the Rio Grande sixteen pueblos on a line sixty miles long.

It is not certain that the inhabitants of the villages around Ascension, for instance, were of the same linguistic stock as those about Janos. In New Mexico the former village of the Queres of Santa Ana was only five miles from the most northerly pueblo of the Tiguas near Bernalillo. Jemez is eight miles from Zia, and each village speaks a distinct tongue. Neither is it certain that the towns were all coeval. As a rule, if we divide the total of ruined pueblos by fifteen, we obtain a still exaggerated figure for the number of those that were occupied at one and the same time, for traditions are abundant and sufficiently explicit to prove how easily the sedentary Indian removes from one site to another, and on what slight provocation. The number of ruins dotting the course of the Casas Grandes River is not, therefore, positive evidence of a large population at any given time. Nor, with all the natural resources of the region, could a considerable Indian population support itself with the aid of stone implements and without beasts of burden.

The cluster of buildings called Casas Grandes par excellence is remarkable for its good preservation and its size. It is difficult to examine all the structures, since modern houses have been constructed on and from several of the mounds. However, to anyone familiar with the aborigines and their mode of life it will become clear at once that the place could not have harbored over four thousand people. The ruins show at least six huge mounds, each of which was a tall house three or four stories high, with walls as thick as five feet, made of what Mr. Cushing has quite appropriately termed "basket adobe-work." The wall is formed by rows of poles bound together by a trellis of branches (of ocotilla mostly), and the space between filled with soil firmly pounded. A plastering of the same material covered both outside and inside, and a wash of gypsum, sometimes painted red, was applied besides. This basket work enables the Indian to make his walls very thick, and thus to rear tall edifices without the innumerable partitions of the northern pueblos. It was an architecture combining purposes of defense with that of abode, and allowing for the exigencies of a warmer climate by making the rooms larger and higher, with a corresponding increase in the size of the doorways and air holes. In one place I noticed what may possibly have been a wooden staircase. The roofs are preserved in some places on smaller edifices, as well as the holes of the beams that supported ceilings. It was the so-called pueblo roof—round timber fastened in the wall and covered with transverse poles, then with brush or grass, finally with earth well pounded and smoothed over.

The great structures at Casas Grandes are so close to each other as to seem contiguous, but it is evident that each stood by itself, narrow alleys separating them. There is no regularity, as in the northern pueblos; it was simply a cluster of tall, clumsy edifices huddled together on a comparatively limited space. Smaller buildings, one-storied and containing from three to a dozen rooms, are scattered along the bases of the high mounds, but they are not so numerous as to lead to the inference that the bulk of the people occupied them. On the contrary, the many-storied houses constitute by far the principal portion of the settlement. From this, and from the fact that all sorts of household utensils have been and are constantly being taken out of them, it must be inferred that they were dwellings, not temples or palaces, and that the smaller buildings (as is the case of the pueblos of today) were houses constructed by such as no longer found room in the main structures, or were occupied by the outcasts, who, for some crime or other, were not tolerated any longer with their clans, or possibly both. For so-called summerhouses, such as the Pueblos of today occupy on their fields, they are too close to the place, nor do they seem to have served for religious purposes.

There is no trace at Casas Grandes of the circular estufa, that semireligious, semisocial architectural feature of the pueblos. Nothing has as yet been noticed that would indicate an edifice for purposes of worship. Fetishes have been found, however, among which I saw and copied (the painting is now at the Vatican) a fetish of the panther or puma, closely resembling those in use among the New Mexican Pueblos. One very interesting find was made many years ago. In a small room on the first floor of one of the tall edifices a monstrous meteorite was discovered. It had been enveloped in cotton cloth, therefore carefully preserved, and was, when found, of a silvery hue. The cloth covering crumbled as soon as it came in contact with the air. The stone was carried to Chihuahua, where it still exists. Of its size and weight I could only ascertain that it was very heavy, since it required great effort to remove it.

The artificial products exhumed from the ruins all show a superior degree of skill—not the pottery alone, although it is strikingly handsome. Greater or less perfection in ceramics is due often to local causes only. This is well exemplified in New Mexico. From a characteristic pueblo ruin near San Mateo, pottery was exhumed that will compare favorably with the best of Casas Grandes. Only a few miles away, similar ruins have yielded very inferior specimens. The same thing occurs in the Moqui country, where Ahuatuyba furnishes the handsomest ceramics of northern Arizona, far superior to those of other ruins in its neighborhood. The Indian adapted his arts to what the locality afforded. His commerce was too limited to furnish him with material from the outside in large quantities, for he had no beast of draft or burthen to transport them any distance. There are traces, at Casas Grandes, of aboriginal trade and barter. Shell beads are frequently found, so are turquoises and marine shells. Some of the latter I had determined by specialists: they proved to be from the Gulf of Mexico and from the Pacific Coast. Casas Grandes lies midway between both.

Objects of stone and flint are not uncommon. The stoneaxes which I have seen and copied are not any better made than those of New Mexico. The arrowheads are the same in form and make, but the hand mills, or "metates," are far above anything I ever found as far north as the thirty-sixth parallel of latitude. They are tolerably well squared and finished. I also saw a double "metate" and a stone pestle with the head of a mountain sheep nicely carved on it. Many other stone implements as rude and as clumsy as those elsewhere found, accompany well-executed specimens of the same utensil. The specific Indian trait of character, inequality of workmanship, displays itself at Casas Grandes as well as elsewhere—no uniformity in execution, but on the other hand, in pottery especially, great sameness in the patterns and designs.

It is a very striking fact that, from southern Colorado and Utah down to the twenty-ninth parallel at least, the pottery decorations should show the same symbols, locally or individually modified. These symbols we are well acquainted with from the New Mexican pueblos; we know that the double staircase signifies the clouds; the spiral and the Greek fret, the whirlwind; the forked line, lightning. We know how the rain is depicted, how the sun, moon, stars, the rainbow. The innumerable modifications of each typical form are also known to us. The fundamental decorations on the pottery of Casas Grandes are the same as those of Pueblo pottery and of Pima baskets or Moqui trays. Still, at Casas Grandes and in the Sonoran Sierra Madre, near Huachinera and Baserac, I have met two figures that were new—the heart and the flag. More remarkable yet is the fact that at Casas Grandes pottery is found decorated with human figures in relief. This indicates progress, emancipation from stereotyped models, the creation of new symbols, perhaps. The heart is frequently met with on Zuñi vases, but always in connection with some animal, never alone by itself, as at Casas Grandes. As to the flag, I know of nothing like it in New Mexico or in Arizona.

Still greater progress is evidenced at Casas Grandes in the vestiges of irrigation. The acequia, or ditch, which runs toward the ruins from the northwest, shows traces of filling and of cutting. It is no longer the primitive method of slavishly following sinuosities of the ground in order to avoid obstacles. The ditch of Casas Grandes runs almost straight. It crosses gulches that could have been passed by means of wooden or stone channels alone. It rests on a bed of stones. Hugging the western edge of the great buildings with one of its branches, it winds the other around the east side, and terminates in the Casas Grandes River. Where the western arm approaches the pueblo, it is lined by a chain of artificial eminences, composed almost exclusively of pebbles, and from three to fifteen feet high. Some are rectangular, others circular, and one has the form of a star with four arms of unequal length. Treasure-seekers burrowed in several of these mounds, but found nothing. They were neither fortifications nor lookouts, for the great houses far exceed them in height, and these same houses were the best fortresses that could be devised against an Indian enemy. Places of sacrifice? Possibly; but although I was informed that charred bones and skeletons had been found on one of them, nothing in the sections made by digging or by decay indicates their use for sacrificial purposes. Furthermore, while every part of the ruins abounds with specimens of broken pottery, this is strikingly scarce on these gravel hills; still there is no doubt that they are artificial. On the southwestern edge of the ruins the ditch runs into two circular tanks. Only one ruin, possibly of Spanish origin, is found outside of the ditch. It was a one-story house, with interior court, differing in plan from the other edifices.

# 6

# THE RUINS OF CASAS GRANDES—II

## Adolph F. Bandelier

There are also ruins on the opposite side of the river, but some distance from the main cluster. The Casas Grandes proper are the remains, as already stated, of a group of houses huddled together on the west bank, dominating the course of the stream for three miles about, up and down, and similar to the other ruins scattered along the river. But it was a larger settlement, and is in a better state of preservation. Was it a sort of "capital" for all the others, or perhaps the last refuge of the population previous to its dispersion, annihilation, or exodus? It is very difficult to decide in favor of either of these surmises. There is, however, one point which deserves careful attention. About three miles west of the ruins rises the Cerro de Montezuma, a steep and bald mountain, at least two thousand feet higher than the valley. It is reckoned that three leagues (eight miles and a fraction) equal the distance from the ruins to its top. That top is the culminating point of a sharp ridge or narrow "hogback," with precipitous sides to the west, in some places. On that top, whence a surprising view is enjoyed in every direction, stands an ancient circular watchtower. Its walls, at least two feet thick, are of thin plates of stone. A wall, now crumbling, surrounds it. Inside there appear at least four small compartments. From this watchtower, as from a central point, well-beaten trails descend the sides of the mountain in every direction: toward the east, to the main ruins; to the north and northeast; to the west, where the villages lie on the Rio de Piedras Verdes; and to the southwest and south, toward the ruins on the Rio de Palanganas. It looks as if this watchtower had been erected and maintained for the mutual benefit of the settlements mentioned; as if, therefore, these or a number of them had been flourishing at the same time, and as if a common bond had existed between the larger cluster at Casas Grandes and the smaller ones on either side of the Cerro de Montezuma. I must add that on the crest of that mountain, but below the tower stands a large ruined house after the type of those of Casas Grandes. That house is protected on the side toward the east by a massive and remarkably well constructed wall of stones. Whether this building was coeval or not with the main cluster at the foot of the mountain, it is of course impossible at present to determine.

Admirably fitted for a center of subsistence on a small scale, the region of Casas Grandes could not fail to attract all tribes that drifted within grasp of its superior natural advantages. It did not so much allure the aborigines to roam over its tracts as to settle on them. Its surroundings are not inviting to the marauding savage except in the west where the eastern branch of the Sierra Madre (called Sierra de la Madera de Casas Grandes) rises like an unbroken wall clad in somber green. There he found profusion of game, abundance of limpid brooks and streams, majestic pine forests, and innumerable lurking places. There, for nearly two hundred years, the Apaches had their favorite lairs, harassing the Spaniards to such a degree that twice the latter almost completely abandoned the valleys of Casas Grandes and San Buenaventura. Since the year 1884, in consequence of the late Gen. George Crook's remarkable armed peace mission into the heart of the Sierra Madre, those angels of devastation have been obliged to forsake that splendid region and to leave Sonora and Chihuahua in peace.

I penetrated into the heart of the Sierra Madre thrice in the spring of 1884. It was still dangerous. But although I was unarmed and had only one or at most two Indian guides, we never suffered any molestation. The Apaches were near, but showed themselves not; certainly not out of fear, but they were then on the move to the Arizona Reservation, and any hostile demonstration with as little returns as our persons would have yielded would have been imprudent on their part. So I was permitted to explore and enjoy a considerable portion of these magnificent solitudes, and to investigate the numerous remains of ancient Indian abodes which they contain. A broad plain separates the former hacienda of San Diego, where the Casas Grandes River is formed, from the eastern front of the Sierra Madre. This plain, about ten miles wide, was alive with antelopes. At the foot of the mountains aboriginal ruins appeared again, recalling isolated houses of clay peculiar to the Casas Grandes valleys. Little garden plots, indicated by rows of upright stones, extend on both sides of the Arroyo de San Diego, which here runs out into the plain, soon to disappear in its barren sandy soil. The ascent through the gorge called Puerto de San Diego is picturesque and grand. A strong vegetation crowds the bases of cliffs; thickets of oak, cedar, and pine alternate with plants and shrubs of a more southern flora. Toward the east the view expands unbounded. Far beyond San Diego it stretches, white and dazzling. The higher we climb the more rugged becomes the scenery, the cooler the air. At last we enter a forest of stately pines, on the first ridge of the Sierra Madre.

It is a great relief, after having for months lived in the hot and dusty valleys, in the glare of a scorching sun, to stroll in deep shade, and to breathe the fresh atmosphere of the mountains. The forest is silent in the evening, but the next morning we are awakened by the chattering of the green parrots in the treetops. Narrow valleys, with tall grass and clear brooks, separate the ridges of pine timber. Flocks of turkeys are seen. Deer make their appearance in close proximity to man; they fix upon him the gaze of their lustrous eyes and saunter off leisurely. We meet the vestiges of huts which the Apaches occupied only a few months ago. Following the Arroyo de los Pilares, we turn into a gorge from which the Arroyo del Nombre de Dios descends. Magnificent pines rise along its banks. Through the array of portly trunks we perceive cliffs, strangely eroded, gigantic pillars, lining the gorge on the south. Numberless small caves open in these rocks. At one place, however, the cavern is quite extensive, and it shelters a small ruined village. Nothing distinguishes this "cave-pueblo" from other ones in the north except the material of which the partition walls are built, and the potsherds, which bear the type of the Sierra Madre and Casas Grandes pottery in general. Such cave homes are found everywhere in the great mountain chain, where the formation is favorable to their construction. Who their builders were we do not know. An old church book of the parish of Bacadéhuachi in Sonora conveys the information that as late as 1655 the Jesuit missionaries wont to administer the sacraments to Opata Indians living in caves, where the "enemy" used to surprise and kill or mortally wound them. The Tarahumares of southwestern Chihuahua were cave dwellers in the seventeenth century, and many of them are cave dwellers today. The different types of architecture in the southwest do not correspond to distinct "stocks," still less to "races." There was no "race" or "stock" of "cliffdwellers" or "cave people." The Indian always yielded to the obstacles and inducements offered by nature, changing his style of abode according to circumstances. The Tehuas of Santa Clara (in New Mexico) at one time made the caves of the Puyé, burrowing out of the friable rock a whole village of grottoes. As soon as drought and decay made the place untenable, they again built pueblos in the open air as before. The Queres tell a similar story. It is therefore unsafe to speculate who the inhabitants of the cave villages in the Sierra Madre were, and at what times they may have occupied their troglodyte homes. It is as much a mystery as the name of the tribe who built the Casas Grandes or the other pueblos scattered along the course of the river of that name on the high plain of Carretas and at the Vadio between it and Janos.

Documentary information in regard to Casas Grandes goes back to 1660. The place seems to have been discovered by a Franciscan missionary, Fray Pedro de Aparicio, who found the valley held by a tribe which he called Sumas. They were friendly, and received him with kindness. But his health soon began to fail and he died, to the sincere regret of the Indians. Sumas also lived at Carretas, and near El Paso del Norte. They and their neighbors, the Janos and Jocomes, were enemies of the Opatas of Sonora, and during the seventeenth and eighteenth centuries the history of the Jesuit missions is one sad tale of woe caused by the incursions of these tribes upon Sonoran territory.

The earliest account concerning the Sumas of Casas Grandes represents them as Indians with sedentary inclinations, and not very ferocious. The Sumas around El Paso, on the other hand, always belonged to the most dangerous class of nomads. Strenuous efforts were made to settle them, but with very poor results. This contrast between two branches of one and the same stock is significant, though not easily explained. Which were the primitive branch—the village Indians of Casas Grandes and Janos, or the nomads of El Paso? I believe the former. Still, this is a mere suggestion. What causes me to think that the sedentary branch might have been the original stock is, first, their greater numbers, and secondly, the analogy with the case of the great Apache stock, of which the half-sedentary Navajos form the bulk, whereas the Apaches proper are but outlying bands who have become nomadic through force of circumstances. Certain it seems that the Sumas were not the builders of Casas Grandes. When Fray Pedro de Aparicio went thither, he found them in possession of the valley, but we have as yet no record of any tradition among them touching the origin of the Great Houses. According to the custom of the times, the Spaniards afterward attached the Montezuma lore to the ruins. The mysterious remains of Indian antiquity became "palaces of Montezuma," or one of the "stations" where the Mexican tribes rested on their supposed peregrination from north to south. This manufactured lore has clung to Casas Grandes ever since, although there is no more foundation for it than for a "Montezuma legend" among the pueblos of Mexico. The name and fame of the unlucky war chief of the Nahuatl Confederacy in the Valley of Mexico flitted to the north in the wake of Spanish discovery and colonization. It settled, like an unsteady fog-cloud, everywhere that vestiges of antiquity attracted attention, without offering also a clue to their makers. In 1726, the Brigadier Don Pedro de

Rivera gravely tells us, of Casas Grandes, that the edifices are of hewn stone; that when the ancient Mexicans migrated toward the central plateaux, Montezuma built these "palaces," and that the number of his followers was 600,000. In 1737, Fray Francisco de Arlegui almost textually copied Rivera, extolling the great architectural skill and beauty of the buildings. Subsequent writers did the same and it was left to John Russell Bartlett to give the first unexaggerated description of the ruins. In his "Personal Narrative" the reader will find a sober and careful account of Casas Grandes, accompanied by excellent drawings.

After the death of Fray Pedro de Aparicio, the Valley of Casas Grandes began to attract the attention of Spanish settlers. A number of them established themselves there and at San Buenaventura, and by 1680 the district was producing good wheat, cattle, and horses. It is well known that, when Governor Otermin retreated from Santa Fé to El Paso with the remnants of the Spanish colonists driven out of New Mexico by the Pueblo Indians, the supplies that saved his famished people were furnished by the settlers of Casas Grandes. That valley was much more prosperous than El Paso del Norte. But the war cloud rising in the north spread into Chihuahua and Sonora, and the Sumas, Janos, and Jocomes joined hands with the Apaches, who were then hovering along the confines of Chihuahua. In the fall of 1684 a secret conclave of all these and more southerly tribes met at Casas Grandes. A general uprising against the Spaniards was planned and partly carried out. The incursions of the Apaches continued thereafter uninterrupted, and they so harassed the ill-protected settlers that forty years later the place was deserted. The Church of San Antonio, the walls of which are still standing one mile north of the present village, was abandoned. The Sumas scattered, the Janos and Jocomes merged into the Apaches. The latter became the terror of Chihuahua. For one hundred and sixty years they held the Sierra Madre and devastated the valleys at its feet. Casas Grandes was settled again, but the present dilapidated condition of the village, the timid and indolent manner of its inhabitants, are the products of a long period of daily perils and of utter hopelessness.

As in New Mexico, so in Chihuahua, the feeling of helplessness has created what we are sometimes too prone to ascribe to natural faults of character or to a lack of education. The latter, of course, has been a factor also, for in the Southwest education had become almost impossible. Spain was no longer able to protect provinces so distant and of such difficult access. The church lacked means and power to continue its work with the necessary vigor. Not unfrequently, also, the local authorities directly opposed its efforts. The Indians relapsed into their original condition, to their own detriment. The tale of the Southwest in the past and present century is a sad tale—one of superhuman efforts (principally by the church) under the most disheartening circumstances. The modern history, also, of Casas Grandes is deeply stained with blood. For four years peace has reigned at last. The beautiful interior of the Sierra Madre becomes accessible. Casas Grandes is no longer a dangerous point. With the general progress now going on in new Mexico, we may expect its archaeological features soon to become the object of research under the patronage of the Mexican government.

## PART 4

# INTRODUCTION

In the 1880s the great natural historian Adolph F. Bandelier published several papers on the early Spanish penetration into the Southwest. Bandelier had become interested in the initial Spanish exploration of New Mexico and Arizona as early as 1880[1] and a visit to Frank Cushing at Zuñi in 1884 added greatly to his interest, especially in the Coronado group—Marcos de Niza and the black adventurer, Esteban.[2]

Bandelier was by the mid-1880s deeply involved in writing up the results of his archival studies and in-person investigations of Southwestern Indians, and archaeological sites. This field and archival work would mainly appear in the two-volume *Final Report*[3] and in the manuscript *Histoire de la Colonisation et des missions de Sonora, Chihuahua, Nouveau-Mexique et Arizona jusqu'à l'année 1700* sent to the Vatican in 1887 and lost for many years. Father Ernest J. Burrus discovered the *Histoire . . .* in 1964 and, parenthetically, began publication of it in an English translation in 1969. The short articles and the longer *Outline of the Documentary History of the Zuñi Tribe*, should all be viewed in the larger context of these major works.

The "Marcos of Nizza" article (published in 1886) is one of the best early attempts to establish the route of Marcos and to test the veracity of his story. Already, in Bandelier's time, doubts were being thrown on the account although the major attacks on Marcos did not come till much later.[4] It might be said here that the exact route of Marcos and the distance he *really* covered are still very open to controversy. The identification of towns and Indian groups along Marcos's route up the West Mexican coast are vigorously disputed and, in fact, we may never know the full truth of the matter. Bandelier's identification of the Indians who traveled with Marcos as Pima is generally accepted today,[5] and his figures for the speed of Marcos's march command confidence for Bandelier, himself, had walked much of the Southwest in his own diverse research and so was a good judge of speed over difficult terrain.

There is one part of the Marcos paper that now definitely seems to be incorrect. The statement in Bandelier that Fathers Pedro Nadal and Juan de la Asunción made an exploratory trip in 1538 (a year before Marcos) and actually reached the Gila or Colorado River is based on a confused statement of Fray Toribio Motolinía later followed by Fray Gerónimo Mendieta and certain still later accounts. As we have seen in a consideration of Bandelier's paper on Juan de Padilla[6] names, times, and places were apt to become very confused in the first century of Spain in America. Carl O. Sauer has suggested[7] that the stories of earlier friars entering the Southwest are simply garbled accounts of Marcos's own trip and the present evidence seems to bear this out.

# 7

# THE DISCOVERY OF NEW MEXICO
# BY FRAY MARCOS OF NIZZA

## Adolph F. Bandelier

The tale told by Cabeza de Vaca and companions[1]—of their wanderings through the Southwest, attracted attention, but it was not necessary in order to stimulate Spanish advance toward the heart of North America. Such an advance was already in progress since 1529, although it had not reached yet beyond southern Sonora. Confused rumors about a vast river flowing into the Pacific Ocean (Lower California was yet deemed an island) were gathered by Spanish outposts. That river was the Colorado of the West.[2]

The tribes of central Mexico knew nothing about the north, beyond that it was inhabited by fierce and savage tribes, and that somewhere in that northern country they themselves had possibly originated. The great quadrupeds of our West were unknown to them. One author affirms that, in 1530, Nuño de Guzmán, then ruler of New Spain, heard of seven towns, lying forty days north of New Spain, and which were rich in gold and silver. That story, it is said, prompted him to undertake his famous expedition to Sinaloa, and occasioned the spread of Spanish arms beyond the Mayo River.

It should not be overlooked, that the story of the "seven cities," was in a measure of European origin. Even prior to Columbus, the tale of the island "Antilia" to which a Portuguese bishop fled with some Christians in the ninth century and where he founded seven settlements, circulated among cosmographers. It was a church legend. The discovery of the Antilles established that the seven cities were not there, but the story was not forgotten, and the mainland appeared vast enough to harbor, in some unknown nook, remnants at least of the legendary towns. Public mind was, therefore, prepared to find them.

The stimulus given to Spanish enterprise by the relations of Cabeza de Vaca did not arise so much from the fact that they conveyed startling intelligence. But the adventures confirmed, in a measure, beliefs previously entertained, thoughts long harbored. Whether the fixed abodes which they had seen, still more considerable ones of which they had heard, lay in the very distant north or in some other direction, the fact of their existence sufficed. But above all, it was considered that among those few men who had suffered so much, and had acquired such intimate acquaintance with country and inhabitants, one at least might prove invaluable as guide to further exploration. Such thoughts at once pervaded the mind of Don Antonio de Mendoza, viceroy of New Spain, and one of the greatest administrators America ever possessed.

The three Spaniards were unavailable. They returned to the mother country and Estevanico the Negro, alone remained. Before however an expedition was started the viceroy cautiously determined to reconnoiter the country, with smaller apparatus, less risk of lives and minor expenditure. No better scouts could the Spanish administrator secure than missionaries of the church. They were wont to risk everything, to penetrate everywhere, regardless of danger. For one who perished, many were eager to follow. Such men could be implicitly trusted; they harbored no afterthought beyond the crown of martyrdom, which was their most glorious reward.

Ere the Negro could be associated with any enterprise, it was prudent to test the truth of his statements. In 1538 two monks, Fray Pedro Nadal and Fray Juan de la Asunción, traveled north as far as the Gila (or the Colorado) River, but returned, being unable to cross it. They had started in January and came back the same year. This was the discovery of Arizona.

Meanwhile, Don Antonio de Mendoza had cast his eyes upon another friar whom, he thought, would be specially fitted for an arduous task like the one northern explorations implied. Fray Marcos of Nice, in the duchy of Savoy, had acquired considerable experience in Peru, Quito and Guatemala. He resided in Mexico since several years and was highly esteemed. To him the viceroy committed the enterprise, giving him as chief guide, the Negro Estevanico, and several Indians of the lower Pima tribe, who followed Cabeza de Vaca into northern Sinaloa. Those Indians had been brought to Mexico and taught the Spanish language on purpose that they might afterward serve as interpreters and introduction with unknown Indians.

Elaborate instructions were issued to the Franciscan monk in writing, those instructions speak highly in favor of the viceroy's perspicacity and tact. As an evidence I merely refer to the following sentences:

> You shall always seek to travel with the greatest possible safety, to inform yourself of whether the natives are at war with each other. You shall avoid giving them any occasion to harm your person, lest it might

compel to proceed against, and to punish them, in which case, in place of doing them good and enlightening them, the contrary would arise.

You will take the greatest care to note the strength of the people, if they are numerous or not, if they live scattered or together, the appearance of the country, its fertility, climate, trees, plants, wild animals, the nature of the soil, if dry or traversed by rivers and whether those rivers are large or small, the stones and metals which that soil contains. If you can secure samples of all these objects, bring them along, or send them, in order that His Majesty may become thoroughly informed.[3]

Thus instructed—confirmed subsequently by a formal power and authorization of Fray Antonio de Ciudad Rodrigo, Franciscan provincial (which document bears date: Mexico, August 27 [old style], 1539), Fray Marcos left San Miguel de Culiacán (Sinaloa) on the 7–19 of March 1539. His companions were a lay brother of the Franciscan order called Onorato, the Negro Estevanico, and a number of well-trained Indians. The Negro was instructed by the viceroy, "to obey you in all matters as if you were myself. Should he fail to do it, he would render himself liable to the punishments inflicted to persons guilty of disobedience against officers invested by His Majesty with the right to command."

Well treated by the few Indians who occupied the country, the missionary reached Petatlán, on the confine of Sinaloa. In that village he remained three days and here Brother Onorato, having fallen sick, was obliged to return to Culiacán, while Fray Marcos, the Negro, and the Indians moved onward, traveling so far constantly near the coast. He now moved among natives belonging to the Yaqui stock. The country was thinly settled, sometimes uninhabited. The people told him that, four or five days beyond and inland, there were large towns whose inhabitants dressed in cotton. He showed his informants specimens of various metals which he had taken along. Their attention was at once attracted by gold which they pointed out saying: that the inhabitants of those settlements had bowls, also nose and ear pendants, made of that material.

After moving for three days among people who received him in the most friendly manner, he arrived at a considerable village called "Vacapa." This was in all probability "Matape" of today.[4] At all events it was about the center of the present state of Sonora, and its inhabitants were "Eudeves." Here he resolved to send the Negro ahead with directions to explore the country north of it for fifty or sixty leagues (135 to 162 miles). "I convened with him that if he learned of populous, rich, and extensive countries he should not advance any farther, but return in person or dispatch me some Indians with a token which we had agreed upon. In case that country was of ordinary size, he was to send a white cross of a hand's length, if more important the cross was to be twice that size, and if it was larger than New Spain the sign was a large cross." Estevanico left in the afternoon of Passion Sunday, and very soon Fray Marcos received a message from him in the shape of a cross or crucifix as high as a man. The Indians who carried it urged the priest to start after the Negro at once, since the latter "had found people who spoke to him of a country, the biggest in the world, and he had with him Indians who had been there." One of these came to Vacapa with the others, and the substance of his tale was, that thirty days' march from the place where Estevan remained (about two journeys north of Vacapa) the first town of a country called *Cibola* was to be found. He further said that "In this first province there are seven cities, very large ones, who all belong to one sovereign. There are large houses whose terrace walls are of masonry, the smallest are one story high with a terrace, there are others of two and three stories, and that of the ruler has four well-arranged floors. At the doors of the principal houses there are many ornaments of turquoises, which stones are quite common in that country."

Fray Marcos was anxious to leave at once, still he had to wait yet for the return of messengers which he had dispatched to the coast. When these came they brought him shields of "cowhides," very large, and some of the coast people accompanied them. They were very poor, belonging evidently to the tribe of Guaymas,[5] a branch of the "Seris."

Leaving Vacapa two days after Easter Sunday, the missionary entered the Opata country, on the valley of the Sonora River.[6] In his company went three Indians of a tribe living east of Matape, and distinguished by the paint on their faces, chests, and arms. "Relatives of theirs reside in the vicinity of the seven cities." These Indians were Pimas.[7]

While traveling up the Sonora River, (which he found well inhabited) Fray Marcos gathered further information about Cibola. All agreed about the number of turquoises found there, that the people dressed in long shirts of cotton and in cowskins; the Opatas themselves owned greenstones and robes of cowhide which they acquired by trading at Cibola. "They added, that besides the seven cities, there were three other kingdoms called Marata, Acus, and Totonteac." But however earnestly the priest followed in the wake of his Negro guide, the latter, disobeying orders, never stopped to wait for him, eager to reach Cibola first, regardless of the commands of the viceroy, Estevan, gradually increased the distance between him and his superior, limiting himself to messages urging the friar to greater haste.

The gray cloth in which the monk was dressed attracted the attention of the Opata Indians. They told him that at Totonteac there was much of the same material, made out of the hair of animals as large as the two small greyhounds which accompanied the Negro, and that the people dressed in that cloth.

The friar's route was constantly to the north. Beyond Bacuachi he left the Opata settlement behind and, entering a region which though, uninhabited, was by no means a waste, crossed the Arizona line of today. After four days of travel through this deserted country, reaching the valley of the San Pedro River, he fell in with the villages of the Sobay-puris;[8] a branch of the northern Pimas.[9] Here Cibola was almost a household word, and he received further information. It was stated:

(1) That the chief place of Cibola was called "Ahacus." (2) That Totonteac lay to the west of the "Seven Cities." (3) That there existed another "kingdom" named "Acus." (4) That Marata was south of Cibola, and that its power had greatly decreased on account of war with the people of the "Seven Cities."[10]

This information he obtained from an old man, a fugitive from Cibola, who dwelt among the Sobaypuris in southeastern Arizona. The last village of these people, the priest estimated to be 112 leagues (308 miles) north of Vacapa; beyond lay a desert which it required fifteen long journeys to traverse until Cibola was reached.[11]

On the 9–21 of May he began this last painful march. On the first day he had to cross a river. Then followed eleven days more through an uninhabited country with abundance of game. It was consequently about the second of June 1539, that he was "met by an Indian, son of one of the chiefs who accompanied me, and who had followed Estevan, the Negro. His face was all dejected and his body covered with perspiration; his whole exterior betokened great sadness." He indeed told a frightful tale, too often repeated to need detailed mention. Estevan had reached Cibola and its people had killed him.[12]

It was a terrible blow to Fray Marcos of Nizza. At the very threshold of the promised land, entrance to it was forbidden by the unexpected hostility of its inhabitants. His own Indian companions refused to go further, they rebelled against his weak authority. The course of prudence would have been to yield to their determination and turn back, but mindful of the instructions of the viceroy, Fray Marcos cut the cords which bound the boxes containing cloth and objects of exchange, and inviting his escort to help themselves, beseeched them to take at least one step further, enabling him to catch a glimpse of the "Seven Cities," and thus report to the viceroy in what he had actually seen.

His inducements prevailed. Even at the risk of their lives the whole party moved on toward Cibola. On their way they met two of the companions of Estevan. They arrived covered with blood and wounds. Here his Indians again refused to go further, and even decided to kill him, but he succeeded in appeasing them and finally came in sight of the desired place. "It is built in a plain on the slope of a hill of round shape; it appears very pretty; it is the most important that I have seen in these countries." He noted that the houses "were built as the Indians had told me, all of stone, of several stories and covered with terraces. This town is more considerable than Mexico; several times I was tempted to go into it, for I knew I was only risking my life which I had offered to God the day I began my journey. At last, considering the danger, I feared that if I should be killed, the knowledge of the country might be lost." So he limited himself to take formal possession of "the seven cities, the kingdoms of Totonteac, Acus and Marata," in the name of Don Antonio de Mendoza, erected a cross, and left, regretfully, though hurriedly.

The return was a flight. The Sobaypuris were angry at the death of their relatives at Cibola and received him with marked unkindness. Only among the Opatas he felt safe again, and further on he thought of reconnoitering the towns of which he had heard in southern Sonora as being inhabited by the people who knew and used gold. From the neighborhood thereof he observed, "seven villages of reasonable size and tolerably distant, a handsome and very fresh-looking valley, and a very pretty town whence much smoke arose. I learned that there was gold in quantity, that the natives manufacture bars, jewels for the ears, and little scrapers out of it." Here also he planted two crosses and took formal possession. On the 2–14 of September 1539, Fray Marcos handed in his official report, written on nine leaves or sheets of paper, consequently he must have returned to Mexico already in August, if not in July, of the same year.

On the strength of the official report, about whose genuineness there is not the slightest doubt, Fray Marcos of Nizza, has been, since more than three centuries, repeatedly accused of cowardice and of mendacity!

The accusation of cowardice is too silly to merit much attention. In not persisting to enter Cibola, the friar acted faithfully and judiciously. He exposed his person enough during the whole journey to show that he was true to his mission, to the letter and spirit thereof. The simple words: "I feared that if I should be killed, the knowledge of the country might be lost," explains his action and justifies it.

Now to the question of veracity. There is no doubt but that the Franciscan monk reached Cibola, for the following year he accompanied Francisco Vasquez Coronado thither. That commander took the route which the friar led him, and arrived safely and swiftly. But once there, the Spaniards grew angry at the priest, charging him with having grossly misrepresented the state of the country, enormously exaggerated both resources and culture of its inhabitants. Therefore, Fray Marcos must have been a great liar and deceiver. He retired to Mexico, and his order honored him for what he had done.

*Where was Cibola?* The name furnishes no clue. There is "Civon-aroco," the "rock where people slide or fall." In the Opata idiom, there is "Chiva-no-ki," the house of Civano, in the Pima dialect of Arizona, and the proper name of Casa Grande. But Casa Grande was abandoned long before the sixteenth century. There is "Shi-wa-na," the name by which the Zuñi Indians designated their home, their tribal range. In 1583, Antonio de Espejo positively asserts: "Zuñi, which the Spaniards call Cibola." Mr. Frank Hamilton Cushing, whose model ethnological researches have thrown such a flood of light on the Indians of New Mexico, and on Zuñi in particular, has determined that in the sixteenth century the Zuñi tribe dwelt in seven villages. Six of these are named in an official Spanish document of 1598. The statement that Cibola was Zuñi is repeated after 1583!

It must be remembered that Fray Marcos always tramped as near as possible due north. We have followed him from the Culiacán to the Yaquis, to the Pimas of central Sonora, the Opatas of northern Sonora, into the valley of the San Pedro in Arizona, to the banks of the Gila River, where he camped. Thence, fifteen days of march would bring him to Cibola.

In the sixteenth century, only two groups of Indians, dwelling in houses of stone and mud, lay north of the Gila: the Moquis of Arizona and the Zuñis of western New Mexico. All the other "Pueblos" were far to the northeast. In a straight line, the Moqui villages are only about 185 miles from Fort Thomas, where the friar probably forded the river Zuñi, only one hundred and sixty. But the straight line is utterly impracticable, even for Indians. The shortest trip from Zuñi to the Gila is about 240 miles, if we take Fort Thomas or "San José del Pueblo Viejo" as terminal point. On his flight, Fray Marcos made at most 10 leagues (27 miles) daily. During the advance, when he proceeded cautiously and slowly, with Indians carrying on their backs casks and bales filled with goods for exchange, 15 to 18 miles would be a good average. It could have brought him to Moqui as well as to Zuñi.

Aside from the fact that the Indians of Sonora, trading as they did periodically with Cibola, would, in case of going to the Moqui village, scarcely have passed Zuñi unnoticed—the report that a similar cluster, called Totonteac, lay still to the *west* of Cibola, points to Zuñi, and not to the Moqui settlement. In the following year the Spaniards visited "Tusayan," west of Cibola, and thence reached the Colorado River, but found no villages between that river and the former. No Pueblos existed west of Moqui in the sixteenth century. Totonteac is an old word in the Zuñi idiom.

South of Cibola, Marata was another tribe, similarly organized, but in a condition of decadence from war. Marata, as Mr. Cushing has ascertained, is properly "Ma-tya-ta," and is the Zuñi name for the group of Pueblos around the salt lakes *south of Zuñi*, whose well-preserved ruins are still visible. These villages lay abandoned in 1540, but it must be considered that Fray Marcos reports, not from ocular inspection, but after the story of an old fugitive who probably spoke of times long past. Still, the fact is interesting as intimating when and how the Pueblos at "el Carrizo" were given up.

"Hacus" is Acoma, the nearest Pueblo east of Zuñi. Its proper name is "A-qo," the Zuñi call it "Ha-cu-quin," the Navajos, "Hacu." "Ahacus," designated as the largest Pueblo of Cibola, reappears under the name "Aguascobi," as the principal Zuñi village—in 1589. It is the "Aguico" of Espejo, the "Havico" of Fray Geronimo de Zàrate-Salmeron,—the "Ha-vi-cu" of the Zuñi Indians, whose ruins are still visible at the hot springs, fifteen miles southeast of the Zuñi Pueblo.

All this points strongly to Zuñi as the Cibola of old. It also indicates that, so far, Fray Marcos, allowing for the insufficiency of his sources, is *singularly reliable.*[13]

The description of the houses applies perfectly to the many storied, terraced, Pueblo buildings. The custom of laying in the frames of trap doors with small turquoises prevailed at Zuñi in former times, as Mr. Cushing has found out. The Zuñi dressed in cotton and had buffalo robes, which they obtained plentifully through trade. Turquoises they always had in abundance, and as there was a communication between Sonora and the north, the statement of Fray Marcos: that the Opatas and Sobaypuris wore them, is very rational and highly probable. Indian commerce goes slow but reaches remarkably far.

The cloth, woven from the hair of the quadrupeds about as large as small greyhounds, and worn at Totonteac, can be found today at Moqui. It is no cloth, but a heavy blanket, woven with strips of *jack rabbit* hair wound around a core of Yucca fibre. That garment was abundant at Tusayan and even at Cibola when Coronado reached the latter place.

Lastly, we come to a statement which seems to place the mendacity of Fray Marcos beyond the possibility of palliation or doubt. It is his assurance: that Cibola was larger than the city of Mexico. But how large was Mexico in 1539? The Indian settlement had been destroyed in 1521; its ruins even were obliterated. The Spanish town sprang up in 1524, and it is questionable whether in 1539 it had much over one thousand inhabitants. A many-storied Indian Pueblo always looks, from the distance, twice as large as it really is, and even if Mexico had two thousand souls, the comparison, far from being exaggerated, was very proper and truthful indeed.

When Coronado captured Cibola in the succeeding year, the largest Pueblo of the seven was called "Maçaqui." The ruins of "Matzaki" lie four miles east of the present Zuñi village, at the foot of the high mesa. The place was inhabited until 1680, then permanently abandoned.

In view of all these facts, it appears absolutely certain that Zuñi was the Cibola of the sixteenth century, of Fray Marcos and of Coronado.

But where, in which one of the Zuñi villages, was this Negro Estevan killed? Mr. Cushing tells the tale. There are two traditions to that effect among the tribe. One relates that the first "Mexican" whom they saw was accompanied by two dogs, that his greedy insolence angered the people and they did away with him during the night. The other, more positive one, was that a "black Mexican" arrived at the Pueblo of "Caquima" and was killed there for his outrageous conduct. Soon after the "Mexicans" came in numbers and made war upon the Zuñis. Estevan had two dogs with him, he was black, and the year after his death Coronado took Cibola by storm.

Caquima lies in a niche of the southern slope of the great mesa of Zuñi, and is plainly visible from the south side only, whence Fray Marcos approached Cibola. His description of a plain—a hill or height on whose slope the village was built—agrees completely with Caquima, as it is seen from a distance.[14]

It is noteworthy that Fray Marcos never mentions mineral wealth in connection with Cibola—Zuñi; only Turquoises. When he mentions gold, it is only in southern Sonora. He speaks of it from hearsay, and may have been deceived. The Indians judged of the metal by its looks, and not after qualities unknown to them.[15]

Cabeza de Vaca never having trod New Mexican soil, Fray Marcos of Nizza must stand in history as the real discoverer of New Mexico, and of its Pueblo Indians. Long mistrusted, often criticized, assailed, nay defamed, he appears at last as a courageous, devoted, sagacious, and thoroughly truthful man.[16]

PART 5

# INTRODUCTION

In the Third Mesa Redonda, held in 1943, the ethnologist Ralph Beals made a number of speculations on the relationships of the north Mexican area and the Southwest. In this paper Beals redelineates the area and includes the Cora and Huichol because of a series of point by point relationships—sand painting, prayer sticks, ritual use of corn and cornmeal among others that they share with the Southwest. Beals also stressed the possibility of Pima-Tepehuan connections (now reasonably well demonstrated).[1]

Beals considered the Cahita to be most closely related to southwestern peoples but without any strong localizations of the relationships. Curiously, he fails to mention the Opata who may have been most closely related of all.

Beals suggests that the term "Greater Southwest" be utilized for this large area with the understanding that it refers to the Southwest of North America not of the United States of America.

In a second paper at the same conference Beals specifically speculated on the relationships between Mesoamerica and the Southwest.

He found on the whole that, while there were many similarities, these were for the most part generalized and elusive. In those cases where highly specific elements or complexes occurred, they were placed in different ritual or other settings in the two areas.

On the basis of his overview, Beals suggested that there may have been four periods in which expansive Mesoamerican cultures affected the Southwest. Translating these into more modern terminology, there is the Early or Middle Formative, (the present trend is to make La Venta, at least in part, Early Formative) the Classic, the Postclassic Toltec period and the Aztec periods of central Mexico. Beals does not, in fact, suggest that direct influences from any of these periods reached the Southwest, but that a kind of cultural "domino effect" may have been at work.

In the light of our present knowledge, Beals's approach seems unnecessarily conservative. Certain lines of evidence that he suggests—for example, that of the botanical evidence—may have been given disproportionate weight in Beals's mind. On the other hand, Beals's long familiarity with northern Mexico led him to point to that area as one that might help clarify Mesoamerican-Southwestern relations.

By strongly advocating the concept of the "Greater Southwest" he included various ethnic groups of northern Mexico with the more orthodox Southwestern groups. This extension of the Southwest cultural entity southward into Mexico brought, in Beals's words "farming cultures of distinctively southwestern aspect . . . face to face in northwest Mexico over long periods of time with Meso American type cultures." As Beals points out, such a conceptualization of the situation makes known Southwestern-Mesoamerican relationships more understandable and casts serious doubts on the existence of an oft-cited "spacial-gap" between the two culture areas. The importance of this intermediate area is becoming far more obvious as more and more information builds up.

# 8

# CULTURAL RELATIONS BETWEEN NORTHERN MEXICO AND THE SOUTHWEST UNITED STATES: ETHNOLOGICALLY AND ARCHAEOLOGICALLY

## Ralph L. Beals

Discussion of the northern Mexico and Southwest areas is impossible until some definition of the regions is made. In the past, various authors have drawn somewhat arbitrary lines across northern Mexico to indicate the southern limit of the Southwest. Some years ago I published a preliminary definition of the southern boundary of the Southwest which began at the Mocorito River in Sinaloa, crossed the Sierra Madre to the east, swung southward to include the nonfarming peoples of the Mesa Central, turning northward along the boundaries of the Huasteca, and reaching the Gulf at about the Rio Soto de la Marina; in other words, including all of northern Mexico as the term has thus far been used in this conference.[1]

I would be inclined to extend this boundary to include the peoples of the Sierra Madre down to and including the Cora and Huichol in Nayarit and Jalisco, although still excluding the peoples of coastal Sinaloa and Nayarit. I particularly differ from Kirchhoff's inclusion of the Cora and Huichol in his Mesoamerica, a matter I will discuss later.

If this or a similar definition of the southern boundary of the Southwest is accepted, the area of northern Mexico disappears as a cultural unity and remains a purely geographic term. As a tentative hypothesis, I suggest that the areal concepts involved should be reexamined and perhaps renamed. The terms "Southwest" and "northern Mexico" I believe have come to have so many different meanings that it would be profitable to abandon them entirely as appellations for culture areas.

Considering first the term Southwest, we find a multiplicity of usages. To the layman, Southwest often means Arizona, New Mexico, and West Texas. To the archaeologist, Southwest frequently means only the area of the Basketmaker-Pueblo and Hohokam cultures (and sometimes only the manifestations of those cultures found in the archaeologist's own state). Other archaeologists have included most of the Basin (Utah, Nevada, and adjoining regions) and parts of northern Mexico. Some ethnologists have extended the area to include southern California and even larger areas of northern Mexico, but establish the Basin region as a separate culture area. Other ethnologists, while accepting a larger definition, talk about the Southwest as though it included only the modern Pueblos and their immediate neighbors. Until such confusion is resolved, it is futile to talk about the relations of the Southwest with other areas.

The terminological confusion described has two sources. One arises from the difference in time horizons the writers have in mind. An archaeologist is forced to include Utah in the Southwest; an ethnologist finds it impossible to lump the impoverished seed and nut gatherers located in the Basin in historic times with the highly developed Pueblo farmers. Moreover, examining such phenomena as the sand paintings of southern California, the ethnologist finds it impossible to disassociate them from the more elaborate ground altars of the Pueblo, so he puts the Indians of southern California in the same culture area. The archaeologist, on the other hand, finds no parallelism between the impoverished archaeology of southern California and the varied and complex remains of the Basketmaker-Pueblo, and so rejects the areal extension.

Much of the foregoing confusion may be avoided by a system of terminology which takes account of temporal factors. I propose that the first step should be the abandonment of the term Southwest in its entirety. For reasons to be adduced later, I also propose that the term northern Mexico be discarded, at least insofar as it refers to a cultural entity. In place of these terms I suggest seeking a new areal term which will express certain environmental and historical fundamentals. Within this area I suggest additional terms be sought to express historic horizons and regional differentiations, perhaps using many of the present terms but giving them sharper definition.

A suggestion in this direction has already been made by Dr. Paul Kirchhoff in his introduction to the recent edition of Baegert. Dr. Kirchhoff points out the possible existence of two cultural horizons in Lower California and their relationship to the problem of Southwestern culture.[2]

Dr. Kirchhoff also proposes a term which I advance as a substitute for the Southwest, namely "Arid North America" (Norte América Arida). Another possibility is the "Greater Southwest."[3]

The Greater Southwest refers to environmental conditions which can be utilized only by those primitive peoples having a high degree of technological specialization. With only scanty game resources, any primitive nonfarming population is forced to depend upon a unique flora requiring special techniques for its utilization. A very large part of the Greater Southwest may be characterized by a flora in which cactus and mesquite predominate at lower levels, pinyon and juniper on higher elevations. At still higher altitudes with heavier rainfall are islands of pine and fir forest. The most extensive of these islands is the higher Sierra Madre in Mexico. Associated with these types of flora are characteristic assemblages of other plants. All but a few stream border plants possess a high degree of adaption either to very deficient rainfall or to prolonged seasons of drought.

The area of the Greater Southwest from a climatic and botanical viewpoint would include Arizona, New Mexico, West Texas, Utah, Nevada, and parts of adjoining states in the United States. Southern and eastern California in large part would be included. Although presenting a somewhat different flora, it is possible that large parts of central California should be included on climatic and perhaps cultural grounds.[4]

In Mexico, Lower California, Sonora, Chihuahua, Coahuila, Nuevo León, and Zacatecas should certainly be included as should the slightly more humid lowlands of northern Sinaloa and Tamaulipas. In addition, I suspect Durango, Guanajuato, Aguascalientes, Hidalgo, and perhaps part of the state of Mexico should form part of the area.

Turning to the cultural justification for such an area, the evidence from contemporary ethnology at first glance seems entirely contradictory. However, the concept of the Greater Southwest is not presented as representing a contemporary reality, but rather as a region in which similar conditions exist and over which at one time in the past there spread a relatively homogeneous culture or succession of cultures upon a pre-farming level. With such an hypothesis, certain contemporary ethnographic phenomena become more intelligible as survivals of a basic stratum (or strata) of similar culture. Dr. Kirchhoff has invoked this approach on a somewhat smaller scale to explain the distribution of culture elements in Lower California. I venture to suggest that it also explains the numerous parallels found in our scanty knowledge of the nonfarming peoples of Coahuila, Nuevo León, and Tamaulipas with the peoples of the Basin and, to some extent, central California.

Time does not permit me to go into detail, but I will indicate a few probable characteristics of this hypothetical basic culture. Perhaps most significant is the presence of complex techniques for dealing with a large variety of vegetable food sources to form the mainstay of the diet. The core of this complex is the leaching process and the seed beater and seed-collecting tray, plus the use of one dominant tree-borne fruit capable of prolonged storage: the pinyon, the mesquite and, if California be included, the acorn. All the nonfarming peoples of the region are primarily gatherers rather than hunters, sharply differentiating them from the other North American peoples. Other elements are techniques for effectively utilizing the small rodents comprising the bulk of the fauna, social organization necessarily consisting of small bands but with a patrilineal bias, ceremonial emphasis upon puberty rituals, a strong development of witchcraft and magic in place of true shamanism, etc.

Certain obvious objections must be countered at once. The equation of mesquite with pinyon and possibly the acorn (but the inclusion of California is doubtful in any case) is objectionable. I can only counter that any large areal unit has validity only in terms of a continental comparison. Uniformity within an area rarely exists but I feel that the close affinity of the mesquite gatherers of Nuevo León with the pinyon gatherers of the Basin in several aspects of social organization call for some such linkage and are of such a nature as not to be accounted for as merely a reaction to similar environmental conditions.

Without further debating the validity of the hypothesis, I would restate it as follows: that at some period antedating the introduction of farming, the Greater Southwest was characterized by a relatively uniform basic culture, very probably marked by local variations partially induced by difference in various environments.

Into this Greater Southwestern area, farming and other cultural influences penetrated from the south approximately two thousand years ago, giving rise to a considerable number of local farming cultures. Because of existing local differences in the prefarming cultures as well as variations in environmental conditions, these local cultures underwent elaboration in somewhat different directions. The more precise nature of these events I will discuss in a second paper. For the present I wish to confine myself to the original problem of the Southwest and Northern Mexico with special reference to the farming peoples.

In the present state of knowledge, the closest resemblances between farming peoples in northern Mexico and those in the Southwest (using this term in the old limited sense) are between the Cahita of southern Sonora and northern Sinaloa. The Cahita have relationships in two directions, with the peoples of lowland Arizona, especially the Colorado River Yumans, and with the Pueblos.

The material culture of the Cahita peoples has many close resemblances to that of the Yumans. In both cases horticulture depends on the utilization of river-flooded lands by very similar techniques, although the Cahita depend more upon farm products than the Yumans ever did. The dominant Cahita house type evidently closely resembled Pima types. Methods of warfare of Cahita and Yumans were also similar, both in organization, weapons, and methods of fighting. In the field of social organization, the Cahita kinship system closely approximated that of the Yumans, although clans were entirely lacking. The resemblance of kinship systems extends throughout the north Mexican Uto-Aztecans as far south as Cora and Huichol.

On the other hand, other aspects of the nonmaterial culture of the Cahita were most closely allied to the culture of the Pueblos. In the field of kinship, although the system is Yuman in character, terminological similarities occur with other north Mexican peoples and, to a lesser degree, with the terminology of the Pueblos. The resemblances in the latter case are random, i.e., the terminological resemblances are with no single Pueblo group. The Cahita are also Pueblo-like in the weakly developed political structure and in the essentially theocratic organization dominated by religious officials. Striking similarities are to be found in the existence of religious societies and in their organization, as well as in many ritual activities. The behavior of clowns, and the existence of sand paintings, are two impressive instances. In general it may be said that the Cahita resemble most closely the Colorado River Yumans in material culture, methods of warfare, and in the kinship system, while having randomly distributed resemblances to the Pueblos in kinship terminology, social and religious organization, and ceremonial and ritual activities.

At the same time the Cahita also have a number of traits which have been described as characteristic of the nonfarming peoples of northern Mexico. The surround of game by firing the forests or grasslands is a case in point, although this is a very widespread characteristic of primitive hunters, occurring, among other places, among many of the California Indians.

Another type of similarity of some interest is that between the Pima-Papago and the Tepehuane. Although the Pima-Papago participate in many culture traits of the lowland Arizona area, they apparently share a considerable number of traits with the Tepehuane which are not found among their other neighbors. In view of the tentative evidence that Pima and Tepehuane may be little more than dialectic variations of the same language, the resemblances between the two groups may have most important historical implications which are worth further and detailed study.

Most striking of all, perhaps, are the parallels between the Pueblo and the Cora-Huichol. Many of these resemblances have been obscured by the fact that early students of the Cora and Huichol, such as Lumholtz and Preuss were ignorant of Pueblo ethnology and were familiar with the culture and problem of Mesoamerica. Later students, in the main, were not interested in comparative problems.

It is quite clear that the Cora and Huichol use prayer sticks, very similar in construction and purpose to those employed widely by the Pueblo. Lumholtz's unfortunate appellation of "arrows" to these objects has long obscured this fact. Unpublished data collected by Elsie Clews Parsons and myself also indicates many ritual similarities. Smoking to the directions is performed in precisely the same manner as among some of the Pueblos, and many other details not only of a ceremonial but witchcraft appear to be similar or identical. The corn ear fetish is employed by the southern groups, utilizing a hollowed perfect corn ear filled with seeds and ornamented in connection with rituals in Pueblo fashion. Although based on inadequate information, there is some evidence of simple sand paintings among the Cora. The Cora also apparently took heads, kept them in caves or possibly in the strong house or "casa fuerte" and fed them cornmeal somewhat as scalps are fed in some of the Pueblos.

These somewhat random examples I think are sufficient to suggest that some relationship exists between the Cora and Huichol and the Pueblo. Possibly this is not sufficient to warrant including the Mexican groups in a Greater Southwestern area, as I have suggested, for they unquestionably possess many traits of Mesoamerican character. At the very least, however, it seems that Cora and Huichol may have to be considered an intermediate group.

The purpose of these somewhat random comments on similarities between various groups is to suggest that the farming peoples of northern Mexico and the Southwest are interrelated, although obviously possessing many specialized characteristics. In relation to the hypothesis which has been advanced, it is suggested that the various groups represent local variations of what may be regarded, in contrast to other areas, as the farming cultures of the Greater Southwest, representing a later overlay upon the earlier and essentially homogeneous nonfarming cultures of the region. If the hypothesis here advanced is accepted, the problem of relations between northern Mexico and the Southwest becomes the problem of accounting for differentiation within the Greater Southwest. The significance of the differences and similarities within the Greater Southwest is connected with the problem of relationships with Mesoamerica and discussion is deferred until my next paper dealing with that subject.

# 9

# RELATIONS BETWEEN MESOAMERICA
# AND THE SOUTHWEST

## Ralph L. Beals

An important advantage of a round table conference is the opportunity for presenting tentative hypotheses and "hunches" to the consideration of colleagues without being committed to a definite thesis or viewpoint. The following remarks on relations between Mesoamerica and the Southwest must be regarded as representing no more than personal hunches on the subject. I am more emboldened to present these ideas in view of preceding papers, especially those by Brand and Haury, which express somewhat similar ideas from the viewpoint of the archaeologist.

From the standpoint of ethnology the cultures of Mesoamerica and the Pueblos present certain specific evidence of contact and more general evidence of similarity. The major and wholly indisputable indication of contact is provided by the botanical data as to the origin of maize and beans which point definitely to Mesoamerica if not still farther to the South. The botanical evidence, however, does not show whether contacts were direct or through a long series of intermediaries.

On examination, the evidence of cultural similarity proves to be extraordinarily elusive. Stone architecture, pottery-making, village-dwelling, farming—all of these are extremely generalized concepts which, upon close examination, present almost no specific homologous resemblances upon which to build a theory of cultural contact. Perhaps the most striking similarities yet to be demonstrated are the resemblances pointed out by Elsie Clews Parsons between the Kachina cults of the Pueblos and the Tlaloc cult of the Aztecs. Yet even here homologies are rare; moreover, other evidence of contact between Pueblo and Aztec is so uniformly negative as to make untenable any theory of direct Aztec-Pueblo contact. In general, it seems that most of us who believe in a relationship between the Pueblos and Mesoamerica maintain this belief by intuition rather than by evidence.

Here I wish to refer to my previous paper in which I suggested that the old Southwestern area should be expanded into an area of Arid North

America or the Greater Southwest, including in large part what has been considered northern Mexico in the previous discussions in this conference. In terms of this suggestion, the real problem is not one of relations between Mesoamerica and the Pueblos and their neighbors, but a twofold problem of the relations of Mesoamerica with the Greater Southwest and the interrelations between various groups within the latter area.

The Greater Southwest, it has been suggested, represents a relatively homogeneous area with respect to environment and culture on a prefarming level. Referring to remarks made by Dr. Kidder, it should be emphasized that in speaking of a relatively homogeneous culture, I certainly presume that significant local adaptations and differences existed. With the introduction of farming in the Greater Southwest, it is suggested that a considerable number of even more highly differentiated local cultures arose. While farming undoubtedly reached the Southwest from the South, and almost certainly was accompanied by other cultural influences, I do not for one moment assume that the existing cultures accepted the new influences blindly and without change. I believe that there was a large element of selection and perhaps even more adaptation of new elements into existing culture trends and patterns. Such a viewpoint is, in fact, basic to the hypothesis I propose to advance.

Considering first the relations between the various groups within the Greater Southwest with special reference to the farming peoples, it will be recalled that in my earlier paper I mentioned the relations of the Cahita with the Yumans, Pueblo, and other peoples. It was pointed out that the resemblances of the Cahita with other peoples are sporadic, essentially suggesting a random distribution of similarities. Thus ritual features found among the Cahita often have close resemblances, amounting to homologies, with various Pueblo rituals. Often these resemblances are found in isolated details in larger ceremonial contexts. For example, the Yaqui coyote dance is performed by the members of the military society to music supplied by a drummer who sings into a hole in the side of the drum. In the scalp ceremonial of Zuñi a specific incident is conducted by members of the Coyote clan in which the drummer sings into a hole in the side of the drum. Such examples could be multiplied manyfold, not only for Zuñi, but for other Pueblos.

Other types of widespread resemblances are less specific, yet some of them may be significant. For example, among many of the Sierra peoples such as Acaxee and Cora, are references to the "casa fuerte" or strong house. Usually this is described as a fort, yet it is also clear that to some extent it served as a ceremonial structure, being used primarily by the men, and that it was the place of preservation of war trophies. Although structurally quite different from a Puebloan kiva, the data suggest a functionally similar use.

As yet another example, the absence of the Kachina cult in the area between the Pueblo and the Valley of Mexico is bothersome. Yet one of the basic ideas of the Kachina cult is the deification of the dead. It is not without significance, that the Cahita, for example, pay a great deal of attention to the dead, apparently regarding them as permanent members of the tribe.[1]

Without piling up additional detailed evidence, I venture to suggest that the random resemblances found among the farming peoples of the Greater Southwest are primarily due to selective reworking and adaptation of elements belonging to an earlier widespread cultural stratum or series of cultural influences.

One line of evidence for such a series of cultural influences is provided by the botanists, as I have already indicated. Recently the botanist has been able to go farther. Writing in the first number of Acta Americana, Anderson points out that Basketmaker maize is closely similar to modern Pima-Papago maize. The same type of maize still occurs farther south along the Pacific coast and has been tentatively isolated from modern Tarascan maize. On the other hand, maize similar to Basketmaker types is markedly lacking in Jalisco and Valley of Mexico collections. This evidence permits us to assume that maize—and probably other cultural items stemming from Middle America—reached the Basketmaker-Pueblo area well before A.D. 500, probably being transmitted along the Pacific coast of Mexico and originating at least as far south as the Tarascan area. At somewhat later dates beans and cotton—both possibly originating on the Pacific coast drainage of Central America—probably followed a similar route.

It is to be noted that this route implies a transmission via the Hohokam area of lowland Arizona to the Highland Basketmaker-Pueblo area. The priority in time of the Hohokam area has already been advanced by Haury and some phases of Hohokam culture seem in a general way much closer to Middle American cultures than does Basketmaker or early Pueblo culture. At the same time the change in physical type in late Basketmaker and early Pueblo times has not been verified for the Hohokam area and suggests that the possibility of a second avenue of movement out of Middle America may have existed. Finally, the possibility of a primarily local development of Basketmaker-Pueblo culture, stimulated by only a minimum of material culture traits, especially horticultural, and reaching the area through highly indirect transmission, must be acknowledged.

The second evidence of Middle American contact in the Pueblo field is the replacement of Pima-Papago type maize after Pueblo II by types closely related to Mexican pyramidal types. According to Anderson, in unpublished data, Mexican pyramidal is the most divergent of all races of Zea maize and has its center in the Valley of Mexico. As the Tlaloc cult must have been well developed in the Valley of Mexico at this time, the possibility is attractive that the appearance of Mexican pyramidal maize was accompanied by the concepts characterizing the modern Kachina cult. In conversation here at the conference, Dr. Brew has expressed the conviction that at Awatovi the Kachina cult beginning is quite clearly indicated in the changes in pottery and mural painting for the period between 1200 and 1300. Unquestionably, however, the Kachina cult did not obliterate older religious concepts, nor was it unaffected by them.[2]

In general, I am inclined to interpret the random similarities, exemplified by the Cahita, in relation to the foregoing influences from Middle America. I suggest there were at least two major periods of Middle American influence on the Greater Southwest, neither of which reached the extremes of the area but substantially affected only the farming peoples. These periods may have been times of rapid diffusion only, or may have been accompanied by actual movements of people. The Mesoamerican influences may have been partly rejected by some peoples, such as the Yumans, but for a very large area I postulate the formation of a fairly homogeneous culture horizon, particularly for the second of these periods. The various peoples affected by this horizon, however, immediately began a process of local differentiation. Some culture elements survived more or less intact, others were reworked, others abandoned. Some diffused further in pure or altered form; some did not. In this way the sporadically distributed yet often specific resemblances can be accounted for.[3]

Turning for a moment to the problem of Mesoamerica, I again find the concept of little use in discussing relationships with the Greater Southwest except as describing a rather vague geographical entity. Within the Mesoamerican area exists a complex series of regional and prehistoric cultures. I do not believe the Greater Southwest had indiscriminate relations with all of these prehistoric and regional cultures but rather with specific regional cultures existing at specific times. Like Pueblo marriage, the relationships were a brittle monogamy, tempered perhaps by occasional mild polygamy, but they were never promiscuous. Our discussion must remain relatively vague until such time as the sequence of culture and the regional differentiations of Mesoamerica are reasonably well known.

As a source of speculation, however, I should like to observe that in the northern part of Mesoamerica three or four periods of expansive culture seem to be emerging in which similar cultural phenomena were widespread. These seem roughly to correspond to La Venta, Teotihuacán, Tula, and Aztec. The first of these appears to have a dating approximating the appearance of farming in the Basketmaker-Pueblo culture. The second is known to have had slight contacts with the Pueblo culture at about the time of the appearance of a type of maize related to the Mexican pyramidal variety typical of the Valley of Mexico. So far, no correlations with later periods are known.

I do not wish to suggest that La Venta or Teotihuacán cultures ever spread over any important part of the Greater Southwest. I do suggest tentatively, however, that the disturbances and stimulation resulting from their expansion may have led to the spread of related but perhaps marginal cultures along certain avenues of the Greater Southwest to the north, resulting in the establishment of a degree of temporary cultural uniformity over considerable areas.

The final demonstration of the hypotheses advanced in this paper will depend on archaeological and botanical evidence. The ethnological approach merely suggests problems and may be used to supplement archaeological evidence, should it be found. Careful correlations with linguistic studies also need to be made. Not only do we need analysis of the sequence of Hokan, Tanoan, and Uto-Aztekan in the United States and Mexico, but we need to know the interrelationships of subdivisions within these groups. For example, the close relationship of Pima-Tepehuan points to the need of supplementary ethnological and archaeological investigation to determine the time and direction of movement. The significance of the Cahita-Opata-Tarahumara grouping is related to this problem. The precise placing of Cora and Huichol is important also.

Reviewing the principal points made in the two papers presented, I suggest that the term Arid North America or Greater Southwest be substituted for the term Southwest. The Greater Southwest is to be viewed as an area, of as yet undefined extent, in which essentially homogeneous cultures existed in a prefarming period. The introduction of farming altered the basic uniformity of the Greater Southwest, giving rise to greater regional differentiation. For a time, however, considerable areas of the Greater Southwest came in contact with the same large stock of introduced culture elements. Retention of the new culture was selective in different regions and also stimulated regional cultural developments. This process probably was repeated at least once after the introduction of farming. The cultural influences from the south were not derived from Meso-america as a whole without regard to time, but were derived from specific local cultures existing within definite time limits. Implicit in the foregoing is the assumption that the Greater Southwest and Mesoamerica are ad-joining culture areas with a boundary of intermediate cultures fluctuating in time. Whatever the reception of the major hypotheses of the two papers here presented, it now seems clear that farming cultures of distinctively Southwestern aspect were face to face in northwest Mexico over long periods of time, with Mesoamerican-type cultures. This was true in the neighborhood of the Sinaloa River on the coast. It was also true in the Sierra Madre historically and perhaps archaeologically, although as yet the boundary is less clearly defined.

In any case, it seems clear that the supposed spatial gap between the old Southwest and Mesoamerica was a creation of our earlier ignorance.

## PART 6

# INTRODUCTION

As early as 1943 at the Third Mesa Redonda held at Mexico City, J. O. Brew pointed out certain facts about the Pueblo past that he felt needed interpretation. For many years the period of Pueblo IV in the American Southwest has been considered as one of cultural regression. This period, beginning about A.D. 1300, did see the disappearance of Pueblo Indians from certain of the northernmost regions of Anasazi occupation. Brew, however, points out that a more important aspect of the change from Pueblo III to Pueblo IV was that of drastic change in pottery styles and designs and other ceremonial art. From a previous art style which was stylistically static, mainly utilizing geometric designs both in pottery and in murals on kiva walls, there was a seemingly sudden introduction of a myriad of life forms, highly dynamic in conception and in execution. In addition to these changes, evidence of masked dancers and mythological beings appear in the art. This is accompanied by a demographic shift of a very fundamental nature with the appearance of large towns, some of which might even be called cities.

Brew also suggested, as had others at this Third Mesa Redonda (see Beals above) that the Kachina cult, perhaps related to the Tlaloc cult of central Mexico, may have been introduced during, or just before, Pueblo IV times. He does feel that a very considerable modification in this cult took place—if it did in fact come from central Mexico. He closes with a warning that until the situation of Pueblo IV is explained, it would be dangerous to accept uncritically the theory of autonomous development in the Pueblo area.

Since the time of Brew's comments, much new evidence indeed indicates that we cannot accept such a simplistic model for Southwestern cultural growth. It now seems that strong Mesoamerican influence reached the Southwest long before Pueblo IV times, and the manifestations in Pueblo IV that Brew found so intriguing represented one of several major cultural intrusions from Mesoamerica into the Southwest.

We now know that a strong wave of Mesoamerican ceremonialism, whose origins are to be found in central Mesoamerica, advanced up the west coast of Mexico, perhaps beginning as early as A.D. 900. This reached its height in northern Sinaloa in the fourteenth century, advancing to Guasave, and from there apparently across the Sierra Madre Occidental to a strong Mesoamerican outpost (superimposed on an earlier Puebloan occupance) at Casas Grandes, Chihuahua. This wave of ceremonialism was almost certainly carried by a formal organization of Mesoamerican traders-missionaries comparable to the later Pochteca. It seems quite reasonable to attribute the startling changes that occur in the culture of the Southwestern Puebloans at the end of Pueblo III and the beginning of Pueblo IV to precisely this source. Indeed, there are stylistic elements and layout patterns in the Jeddito-Sikyatki ceramics singled out by Brew which suggest very close ties to Mesoamerican ceramics made at this time at Guasave in northern Sinaloa —and these derive very specifically from Aztec I–II, or related cultures in the Valley of Mexico. Brew suggests a focus of this new wave of Mesoamerican influence was the Tlaloc cult. This, in turn, became the cultural stimulus for the strong development of the Kachina cult among the Pueblos during Pueblo IV. The new evidence now available to some degree supports this view.

If the perceptive suggestions set forth by Brew had been more rigorously investigated a few decades ago, we probably now would have a much firmer idea as to the nature, extent, and mechanism of this contact than we indeed have.

# 10

# ON THE PUEBLO IV
# AND ON THE KACHINA-TLALOC RELATIONS

## J. O. Brew

The following statement, considerably expanded herein, was made in reply to a question by Dr. Caso as to whether the retrogression usually attributed to the Pueblo IV period in the American Southwest refers to a degeneration of culture or merely to a restriction of area or to both.

In my opinion any retrogression at that time, approximately A.D. 1300 was in area alone. The terms "Retrogressive" or "Degenerate" Pueblo as previously and even currently used are, I believe, misleading ones which contradict our archaeological findings. The cultural changes which then occurred, as revealed by excavation and by reconnaissance seem to represent a considerable cultural advance rather than a degeneration. Definite and even startling progress appeared in many forms, particularly in art, in religion, and in the size of the towns. It might better be called the Golden Age of the Pueblos.

The most common diagnostic for Pueblo IV is an abrupt and at present inexplicable change in pottery design. The most famous examples of this are the Jeddito Black-on-Yellow and associated Sikyatki Polychrome wares in the Hopi country in northeastern Arizona. The entire character of pottery painting changed. The shift was not only in design, but also in color, painting technique, and in the placement of the designs on the vessels.

In place of the relatively simple and static geometric designs of Pueblo III the new era was dynamic, characterized by sweeping figures, representations of birds (including the parrot), animals, insects, the human hand, and human figures often wearing ceremonial masks. A mere glance over this material immediately indicates a new and vigorous artistic symbolism. Associated with this vital change in design were equally startling developments in painting methods including stippled and spattered backgrounds and "fillers," drybrush techniques, "scratchboard" incising, and a much more liberal use of open, unpainted spaces within the area covered by the designs. The previous geometric designs did not disappear but were retained in somewhat modified form on many vessels and were also used as fillers, on the wings and bodies of birds for example, and as borders for the new figures.

The change in ceramic art was duplicated in the ceremonial mural art. Paintings on the walls of kivas, the subterranean religious chamber of the Pueblos, were almost entirely geometric during the Pueblo II and Pueblo III periods. In Pueblo IV this, too, became dynamic. The birds and other symbols found on the pottery appeared in the wall paintings and many others occurred in addition, including obviously mythological beasts. Human representations and masked dancers were very common, much more so than on the pottery.

It is obviously impossible to enumerate at this time all of the other changes which took place. Perhaps the most striking one not already mentioned is the marked increase in the size of the towns, many of which during Pueblo IV should be more properly termed cities.

Throughout the Hopi country, along the Little Colorado, San Francisco, Verde, Puerco, and Pecos rivers and the Rio Grande and extending southward in Arizona and through southern New Mexico into Chihuahua the enlargement of the towns may be observed. And it occurs not only in the river valleys but on the intervening plateaus as well.

All of this does not seem to me to suggest cultural degeneration.

To answer Dr. Caso's question completely it is necessary to consider for a moment the history of the study of Southwestern archaeology. Much of the early work, from 1874 to 1930, was done in the drainage of the Rio San Juan in northwestern New Mexico, northeastern Arizona, southwestern Colorado, and southeastern Utah. That large and previously important area was definitely abandoned before Pueblo IV and it is from this fact, I believe, that the theory of degeneration in the Pueblo IV times arises. In the light of modern knowledge then, it seems that we must consider the retrogression to have been merely geographical. And it is only fair to state here that some students do not agree even to that, but believe that the loss of area in the north was compensated by expansion toward the south. The latter theory, though not widely held still should be considered.

We now come to the significance and possible interpretations of all this. The meaning of this startling change can not and should not be set down as yet. The traditional attitude of Americanist[s] in the recent past has been to consider the Pueblo IV developments as completely indigenous. They may very well have been so. The mere increase in size of urban centers is generally assumed to call forth greater social and religious activity and to encourage development in the fine arts.

On the other hand, in the presence of changes which are apparently both extensive and abrupt I believe that we should seriously consider the possibility of strong outside influence. Few people believe now that the Pueblos existed in complete isolation and outside influences of limited effect are assumed as a regular part of their developing culture. It is also now considered possible that major outside influences may have arrived occasionally. But from the original introduction of maize to the coming of the Spaniards there is no time more suggestive of important outside influence than in the years around A.D. 1300.

If such influence existed in fact, it probably began during Pueblo III times and may be foreshadowed by the strange Mimbres art of southwestern New Mexico. And if it did exist it seems most logical to look for it to the south. The appearance of masked figures in Pueblo ceramic art and on the kiva murals is most suggestive. Dr. Beals has already suggested to this conference that the Kachina cult of the Pueblos may have been introduced from the south and may have been remotely connected with the Tlaloc cult of central Mexico. Dr. Haury has mentioned the Kachina-like figure found by Dr. Cushing in a cave near Phoenix, Arizona in association with fourteenth-century material. This and many other possibilities should be thoroughly explored.

The problem is not simple. The form and detail of objects uncovered by archaeologists in the Pueblo area can not be duplicated at present in Mexico. If the influences did come from the south they were altered in detail by the Pueblos and adapted to their culture. The Southwestern manifestations referred to above are not obviously similar to Mexican traits as are those cited by Dr. Griffin and Dr. Ekholm in the Southeast. If the Kachina cult came from the south it was modified to fit Pueblo ceremonialism to a much greater extent than seems to have been the case with the "cult" referred to in the Southeast. Our architectural evidence of the step by step development of the kiva from the Basketmaker pit house clearly indicates the antiquity of the basic Pueblo religion. This is further indicated by the unequal distribution of the Kachina cult among the Pueblos.

There are, however, other possibilities to be considered in investigating the theory of Kachina-Tlaloc connections. Some or much of the change from Tlaloc to Kachina may have taken place in northern or western Mexico. Or they may both have developed from some source at present unknown.

We now come to my reason for emphasizing at this time possible Mexican influences in the Pueblos. It seems to me, particularly since the presentation of the Hohokam culture in southern Arizona, that the time is ripe for a serious search for influences from the south in Pueblo culture. And it also seems that one of the most promising periods for a major influence from that direction is at the end of the Pueblo III.

Consequently, I hope that students of the cultures of the Southwest, and of northern, western, and central Mexico will bring forth every bit of archaeological, ethnological, and linguistic evidence they have which may bear on the subject. It is also important that further field work with this point of view be carried out in the areas between the Southwest and central Mexico. Those familiar with the region will know the most promising places in which to look. I believe this to be extremely important, for the situation in Pueblo IV is such that until we have thoroughly explored the possibilities of southern influence at that time, I do not think we can conscientiously accept the theory of entirely indigenous development.

PART 7

# INTRODUCTION

During the last decade or so of the nineteenth century and continuing for a number of years into the twentieth century, the ethnologist-archaeologist J. Walter Fewkes worked in a number of Southwestern areas. He directed major excavations (Mesa Verde, for example) and did a considerable amount of field ethnology, particularly among the Hopi. In the trend of these times Fewkes, like his contemporaries Bandelier and Cushing, was especially interested in interpreting the archaeology of Southwestern peoples in light of their historic and contemporary cultures.

This discussion of the butterfly myths and ceremonies among the Hopi, written in 1910, is rich in implications of historic and prehistoric interchange between the Hopi and the eastern Pueblo areas. After the long years of rather particularistic studies of Southwestern cultures we are, today, turning once again to the broad implications of continuities in time and the meaning (and organization) of contacts within the Southwest and between the Southwest and other areas, particularly Mesoamerica.

# 11

# THE BUTTERFLY IN HOPI MYTH AND RITUAL

## J. Walter Fewkes

The butterfly, moth, and dragonfly, are among the most prominent insects figured on prehistoric Hopi pottery; they are frequently mentioned in the mythology of these people, and their symbols occur constantly on secular and ceremonial paraphernalia. There is a prominent clan in one of the Hopi pueblos called the Butterfly clan which preserves legends of its past history and migrations.

It has been shown in an earlier number of the *American Anthropologist* that there are important modern survivals of a butterfly cult in a nine days' dramatic ceremony called the Owakülti, occurring biennially at Oraibe[1] and occasionally performed at Sichomovi. From the abundance and variety of symbols of this insect depicted on prehistoric objects it would seem that formerly the butterfly played an even greater role than at present in the Hopi ritual.

It is instructive to notice that there has been a radical change in the symbolism of this as well as other life forms, if we compare prehistoric and modern representation of this animal. This change is radical and not one we can ascribe to evolution; the modern symbol is not more realistic than the ancient, nor is it a development from it. Perhaps no figures of animals are better than those of the butterfly to show this change of form, and a comparison of no other series sheds a clearer light on the mythologic and ritualistic life of the Hopi. It has occurred to me that a brief account of the butterfly and its symbolism among the Hopi might aid the student of myths and rituals of other pueblos, especially those of the Keres and Tewa linguistic stocks from which the Hopi sprang. Although the following account must necessarily be brief this does not imply that the subject is limited in scope, for the butterfly cult is not only one of the most complicated but also one of the widest spread in the Southwest.

A clear knowledge of paraphernalia and cult objects used in modern pueblo rites is a great aid to archeological work in pueblo ruins, and a familiarity with legendary history is especially helpful in identifying village sites or determining the clans that once inhabited them. Knowing the objects that survive in the cult rites of any clan a student can recognize them when found in prehistoric ruins and thus interpret their meaning. To indicate the significance of the above statement it is my intention to illustrate this connection of prehistoric and historic ideas and their expression, by means of facts drawn from one of the smallest of the Hopi clans, the range of whose migration, since it came to Hopi, is comparatively well known.

## Migrations of the Butterfly Clan

The migration history of the Butterfly clan of the Hopi is clearly connected with that of the Badger people.[2] Neither of these clans now inhabits Walpi, but next to the Asa the combined Butterfly-Badger clan is the most prominent in a small pueblo called Sichomovi situated on the east mesa of the Hopi, midway between Hano and Walpi. This compound clan is reported to have been one of the latest arrivals in the Hopi country and according to legends the original home of at least the Butterfly section of it was the eastern pueblo region.

So far as we can now reconstruct Hopi clan history the most ancient pueblos[3] near the east mesas were all settled, in prehistoric times, by colonists belonging to the Tewa and Keres linguistic stocks, and the original settlers came from the east; later the villages they founded were enlarged by increments from north and south, but there is good reason to believe that even the Snake clans from the north drifted into northern Arizona from the east following down the San Juan River valley from more ancient homes in southwestern Colorado and New Mexico. The modern pueblo culture of northern Arizona is believed to have been derived from the San Juan and Rio Grande regions; although all its components did not come from these localities. The builders of the great compounds in the Gila-Salt Valley and its tributaries, in the growth of the Hopi pueblos, contributed a distinct type akin to that of the northern states of Mexico.

The first traces of the presence of the Butterfly clans at Hopi, according to legends, goes back to the ancient settlement, Awatobi, discovered in 1540 by Tobar and flourishing in 1583 when visited by Oñate. While we have no historical statement that members of the Butterfly clan lived in this populous pueblo when first visited by Spaniards it is distinctly stated, in legends, that they were there in 1700 when the pueblo was destroyed by the other Hopi villages. Legends rather vaguely intimate that the Butterfly clans were Tewan in kinship, in corroboration of which it may be said that the name *buli* (*poli*), "butterfly," is a Tewan word and presumably of eastern or Rio Grande origin.

Little is known in a detailed way of the migrations of the Butterfly people before their advent in the Hopi country, and their settlement at Awatobi. From their kinship with the Badgers we may suppose that they had a similar origin.

The Badger (Honani) people are intimately associated with the masked dances called Kachinas and are reported to have come from the Rio Grande region at a comparatively late epoch in Hopi history. We know from legendary accounts that this clan formed a part of the population of Awatobi, at the time of the massacre at that pueblo, and that it had a sacred shrine at Awatobi in the plaza near the old mission east of the ancient town. This shrine, now in the National Museum, was excavated in 1892 and was found to contain prayer sticks which the Hopi workmen identified as belonging to the Kachina cult. The walls of the shrine, like those of the Badger or Kachina shrine at Walpi, were made of upright slabs of stone on which were depicted rain cloud symbols the colors of which correspond to those of the four cardinal points.

It is perhaps premature to speculate on the kinship of any of the early colonists that founded Awatobi, but from all that can be gathered I am inclined to the belief that the original settlers were colonists from the eastern region who had migrated hither via Zuñi, Acoma, and other eastern pueblos. It would appear that some of the pueblos near Awatobi on the Antelope mesa were Tewan in origin while others were probably Keresan, as the name, *Kawaika*, indicates. The pottery of Awatobi, Kawaika, and some other ruins on the Antelope mesa is closely allied in symbolism to that of old Sikyatki and Shumopavi. The existence of Butterfly and Badger clans in Awatobi at the time of its destruction (1700) points to a Tewan origin which strengthens the belief above stated that Awatobi, like Sikyatki and Walpi, was founded by eastern clans which later drew to their number other clans of eastern and southern origin. When Awatobi was destroyed by the other Hopi pueblos, the legend declares that the men were all in the kivas and were killed by the hostiles; but the women and children were taken to Maski Skeleton House, now indicated by a mound in the plain, and were divided among the participants in the massacre. All those women who refused to go with the captors were killed, but the others, of diverse clans, were distributed among the villages.[4]

After the destruction of Awatobi the women of the Butterfly clan who survived the massacre were apportioned among the allied pueblos, the majority of them being taken to Oraibe or its neighborhood.[5] They are said to be the ancestors of the present Butterfly clan. After remaining at Oraibe some time they left this pueblo, crossed the intervening valleys, and joined a new pueblo founded shortly before, called Sichomovi. In this new pueblo there were people of Zuñi descent, for which reason it was early called the Zuñi pueblo in "Hopi-land."

The Asa clan that founded Sichomovi is said to be the same as the Zuñi Aiwahokwi but the Hopi claim that its original home was in a Rio Grande pueblo and that it was of Tewa extraction. As the Butterfly and Badger were both from the Rio Grande there was a good reason for the union of the Asa, Badger, and Butterfly clans in the pueblo founded by the Asa. From the sociological point of view we are led to believe that Sichomovi was peopled by Tewa clans and founded by colonists from Zuñi.

The above legends are supported by evidences drawn from ceremonial dances. In January the men of Sichomovi take part in a dramatic rite that celebrates the return of the Kachinas, the personators in which drama represent Zuñi Kachinas and bear Zuñi names; it is universally stated that this is an introduced Zuñi dance, and there are other dances in this pueblo ascribed to the same source. Sichomovi is the only Hopi pueblo that celebrates the Zuñi Shalako, which, although very much worn down and with many episodes omitted, being performed in July instead of in the winter, is still recognizable. These and other evidences might be mentioned in support of the belief that Sichomovi is a pueblo of Zuñi clans now speaking Hopi. We shall presently see that the Butterfly clans have a dance which affords still further evidence of foreign kinship.

The Hopi all assert that the Asa spoke Tewa before they lost their language and that before they migrated to Zuñi they lived in the eastern pueblo region. Old legends mention ruins in which the Asa claim to have lived during their emigration and these ruins are situated in the present Tewa territory. The Butterfly legends also declare their ancestors were Tewa when they went to Zuñi, and that they formerly lived in New Mexico, having later lost the Tewa language and adopted the Hopi speech. The Asa, as elsewhere shown, at one time in their Hopi life went to the Canyon de Chelly in New Mexico where, having intermarried with Navaho, they sojourned a considerable time, at the expiration of which they returned to the east mesa. Before their departure for Canyon de Chelly they inhabited the row of houses north of the snake kiva near the "Ladder Trail," but after their return they founded Sichomovi where the majority of their descendants still live. There are other legends of the Butterfly and Honani peoples of similar import, to consider which would take me too far afield at this time.

## Prehistoric Art Essentially Symbolic, Not Realistic

An examination of prehistoric pueblo pottery from Arizona and New Mexico shows that while there are certain symbols common to all ruins there are others peculiar to individual pueblos. The symbols characteristic of each ruin point to the kinship of the former inhabitants of these pueblos and by comparative methods can be made to bear on the study of the prehistoric migrations of clans. It is evident, for instance, that prehistoric symbols form in a way a primitive alphabet and the appearance of the same in widely separated ruins indicates when rightly studied a former contact of the people.

It is necessary as a preliminary to generalizations regarding symbols to differentiate such as are universal in the pueblo area from those which are more local or found only sporadically outside of certain restricted areas. We must likewise have material from each ruin abundant enough to determine the symbols which predominate in that region but are rare or wanting elsewhere. What are the characteristic symbols of individual clans of prehistoric Hopi, and how do they differ from those of ancient Zuñi, considering each of these regions as a culture area? What symbols do the old Tewa in the Rio Grande valley share with the ancient Hopi villages now in ruins, founded by Tewa colonists from them? An adequate answer to these questions involves an intimate knowledge of the symbolism found in characteristic ruins, and comparative studies of these productions with other extraterritorial paleography. It is desirable for comparative purposes to accumulate a considerable body of picture-writing from many regions of the Southwest before any broad generalization can be attempted. It is also necessary in this research to discover whether any characteristic symbols have been originated by or are associated with certain clans, and what knowledge of their significance can be derived from studies of the survivors of those clans still living in modern pueblos.

At the very beginning of studies along the line above suggested it seemed to me evident that the modern symbolism of Walpi or Zuñi and other pueblos was like the population, composite, and distinctly different from the ancient. Socially and linguistically most pueblos are conglomerate, derived from many clans originating in distinct localities. It has long been recognized that both modern Hopi and modern Zuñi symbolism are very different from the symbolism of prehistoric ruins near the inhabited pueblos. In other words the symbolism changed[6] after these neighboring ruins in which contributory clans once lived were deserted.

This change is regarded as due not so much to evolution as to the incorporation of new elements by incoming clans and the adoption of new symbols from foreigners. It cannot be strictly true that there is an evolution of modern Hopi from ancient Hopi symbolism, but in the case of the Hopi an entirely new symbolism has been introduced from the Rio Grande. This introduced art, which is Tewan, has driven out of existence the production of ancient Hopi symbolic pottery decoration. The same change has taken place in Zuñi symbolism, as is evident when we compare figures on ancient and modern Zuñi pottery; the latter is closer to that from the Rio Grande than the former which is, like that farther down the Little Colorado, derived from southern Arizona.

When a prehistoric pueblo artist drew a figure of an animal on pottery he gave primary attention to the predominating power which he attached to that animal. He thus endeavored to give an impression of action or pictorially indicate what the animal could do. Representation of action is thus one of the main characteristics of prehistoric Hopi art. The power of flight[7] of the bird made a strong impression on the ancient Hopi and the wing and feather were adopted as the best possible symbols of flight. Not only every bird but likewise a flying snake or dragon must in this conception have some representation of wings or feathers; even in insects it is impossible to separate this idea of flight symbolized by the feather from the animal depicted.

Although the Hopi have distinctive names for different kinds of birds and butterflies, figures of the former are distinguished from the latter generally by the possession of feathers. All animals that fly have exerted a marked influence on the religious life of the Hopi and even serpents are endowed with feathers. But conventionalized figures of both birds and butterflies are so made that it is often difficult to decide whether a figure represents a bird or insect, or to distinguish between the form and a moth. The word for one is often used for another, anatomical distinction not being recognized to any extent. Thus the objects on pedestals in front of the Owakülti altar are called birds or butterflies; both are flying beings and, while clans have no distinct names, as individuals each has a distinct name. It is the feather of the bird, its beak and claws, rather than the variation in the bodies that has the distinctive ceremonial importance.

The modern Hopi have two names for the moth and butterfly, of which *hokona* is believed to be the older as it appears in the name of the ancient stone slab that the Antelope priests place on the Antelope altar in the snake dance. The other name, *buli* or *poli*, is Tewan in origin and is that commonly used. The symbol of the butterfly, as shown in modern figures, is not very different from that found in ancient Zuñi ware. We seldom find the figure of a butterfly on the modern Tewa ware made at Hano which has practically taken the place of the ancient.

Hopi butterfly and bird pictures, as has been pointed out in reports on the excavations at Sikyatki and in ruins on the Little Colorado, excel all other animal motives on pottery decorations. Previously to my discoveries at these places the existence of the feather motive on prehistoric pueblo ware had not been recognized, and the presence of birds was known only obscurely. It was then recognized that there is a marked tendency to similarities in symbolism representing flying animals as birds and insects. To depict a flying snake with feathers, although far from realistic, would seem within the range of art, and a figure of a butterfly with bird characters was not regarded as a violation of primitive art although it would shock the realistic ideas of a naturalist. Highly conventionalized bird and butterfly symbols are thus often indistinguishable and grade into each other so closely that they are extremely difficult to separate. Both of these animals are sometimes represented by triangles, a fact which reveals the danger of relying too strictly on the identification of geometrical figures as animal forms. Although the highly conventionalized bird and butterfly symbols are difficult to distinguish it is self evident that figures with four wings are butterflies and not birds. But both butterfly and dragonfly symbols when highly conventionalized resemble each other, both having four wings. The attempt is made simply to represent a flying animal and a closer identification is difficult, if not impossible.

As the first object of the Hopi in drawing a flying animal was to introduce that part particularly associated with flight as a symbol, so with his pictures of the power of other animals, where he likewise chose symbols of action. Thus the antelope constantly has the heart depicted in symbols for it has "good wind," and proper heart action is associated in the primitive mind with endurance in running. The rattlesnake moves in a zigzag course and strikes to kill, both of which powers appear in the crudest figures of these animals.

It seems a far cry from legends to pictographs but in our Southwest they are intimately associated; here as elsewhere pictographs may serve as valuable verifications of migration legends, serving definitely to identify sites of former habitations and thus to prove the truth of traditions. It can be shown that certain pictures on rocks and pottery open new chapters in our knowledge of ancient rites and ceremonies and their derivation.

There are many localities in the Southwest where we find pictographs of butterflies, moths, and dragonflies. The great collection of Hopi pictographs on cliffs at Willow Spring, not far from Tuba, Arizona, may be mentioned as an indication that members of Hopi clans, whose totems are there recorded, once tarried there, possibly in their clan migrations, or in their visits to the Supai or the salt deposits[8] of the Colorado.

## *Moden Hopi Figure of a Butterfly*

[The design described below] representing one of many pictures of butterflies made by modern Hopi, was copied from the back of a helmet used at Sichomovi in 1891 in personations of the Duck Kachina; its presence there being thus explained by the painter: "The butterfly is just as fond of the water as the duck." Several characteristic structures will be noted in this picture, one of the most constant of which is the two appendages to the head, each terminated by a red circle.

The body of the original picture is green in color, the end of the abdomen being pointed and crossed by black lines. This body is spotted with white, black, and red spots, the whole outlined with black. There are four wings spread like those of a moth in repose. The upper wings are white with the middle colored red, and dotted with white, green, black, and yellow spots. The two posterior wings have yellow borders, red in the middle dotted with green spots. Along the lower border of the posterior wings are white margins with black dots. The interior of the anterior and posterior wings has a black margin. As this complicated picture of a butterfly or moth was from a helmet mask in a Kachina dance it may be regarded as embodying the modern conception of butterfly symbolism. Many other modern pictures of butterflies are extant but this is a good one for a comparative study of the ancient representations as found in Sikyatki or the ruins on the Little Colorado.

Let us compare this figure with the symbol of a butterfly from a ruin near Awatobi. Some time before his death the late Mr. T. V. Keam collected from near this ruin several stone slabs which the Hopi identified as connected with one of the ancient ceremonies of that pueblo.[9] These slabs were really the boundary walls of the shrine of a basket dance called the Owakülti, formerly celebrated at that place.

On one side were painted in color, still visible, pictures of rain clouds, and on the opposite, insects identified by the Hopi as butterflies, although in some cases the figures are closer to dragonflies. [In this figure] we see the four outstretched wings of triangular shape, one end of the body being pointed and that representing the head being rounded. On one of the smallest of these stone slabs there are figures resembling dragonflies, two lobes of the head being shown in the figures.

The beautiful Sikyatki-Awatobi pottery is rich in pictures of moths and butterflies, the most remarkable instance of which is the so-called butterfly vase[10] from the former ruin. The number, arrangement, and other features of these butterflies lead me to associate it with religious conceptions concerning this animal that figures conspicuously in Hopi mythology.

We often find lines on bowls from Sikyatki terminated in circular figures or dots from which extend radiated or parallel lines which have sometimes been interpreted as feathers. These dots are sometimes double and often there are one or more perpendicular lines crossed at right angles to the line on which they lie. These dots, parallel or radiate lines, and cross lines, can be interpreted by a design on a fragment of pottery from Sikyatki where occurs a decoration which furnishes a key to their meaning. The figure on this fragment represents a dot and two cross lines at right angles to a line to the end of which is attached an undoubted feather. The dot represents the knot by which a feather is tied to the string and the two cross lines indicate two knots, the whole decoration representing a feather offering called by the Hopi a *nakwakoci.*[11] It is evident that the parallel and radiate lines represent feathers and the enlargement at the end of the string the knot[12] by which the feather is tied. The figures of feathers and notched ornaments at the end of a club-shaped body so common at Sikyatki are limited to true Hopi ruins or to those showing that influence. They are mainly confined to pottery although occurring in pictography as well as on ancient ceramics.

## The Butterfly Dance

The so-called butterfly dance or Bulitikibi of the Hopi is said to have been introduced by the Butterfly clans. So far as known this dance has not been described although repeatedly seen by those visiting several of the Hopi pueblos. It is so closely related to certain tablet dances of the Rio Grande Tewa that it is almost indistinguishable from them. The most important part of the Hopi butterfly dance is the public performance, there being no altars or fetishes and so far as known no important secret rites connected with it. As it is performed in the open plaza it can be seen by all, and to it the Hopi welcome all spectators. Like the Buffalo dance, which I have described elsewhere in the *American Anthropologist,*[13] it may be called an abbreviated dramatic performance, the secret ceremonies having been dropped and lost.

The dance is performed by men and women appropriately appareled, the latter wearing on their heads tablets the edges of which are cut in terraces to symbolize the rain clouds, their flat surfaces being adorned with butterfly, sunflower, and other symbols. There are other tablet dances at Hopi, the best known of which are the Humis Kachina (Jemes "Cachina"), and the Palahikomana, but the butterfly tablet-dance is more like the "tablita"[14] at San Juan and other Rio Grande Tewa pueblos, than either of those mentioned.

I need not enter into an elaborate description of this dance as it is essentially the same as that performed in Rio Grande pueblos described by others. Not only the dance but also the songs and paraphernalia are almost identical.[15] In some of the Balintikibi dances the participants have a banner, not shown in the figure, which is made of cloth on which is painted the head and bust of a Hopi girl, an object given to them by Major Williams formerly the Navaho agent. The presence of clowns in the one recall those in the other, although their performances vary from year to year as has been frequently described. This banner is of course not connected in any way with the ancient ceremony. Among the personages who appear in the butterfly dance at Hopi, the so-called clowns are among the most instructive in their clan relations.

The Hopi have at least three types of clowns, those appearing in this dance being distinctly like those of the eastern pueblos. In order to comprehend the bearing of this conclusion let us consider these Hopi clowns and their possible provenance.

Evidences that the Hopi ritual is a ceremonial mosaic of different cults imported from different regions is afforded by the existence of three kinds of clowns who amuse the spectators in the sacred dances. Each of these three types is associated with a distinct group of clans which has been added to the Hopi population from time to time.

The clowns of the Tewa pueblo, Hano, are peculiar to that village. They are distinguished by alternate black and white bands girdling body and limbs and they wear on their heads a cap with two hornlike projections made of skin to which are attached small bunches of corn husks. Although regarded as priests they have no altar or fetishes, their religious function appearing only in the prayer sticks that they place in certain shrines. These clowns closely resemble those of the Tewa villages on the Rio Grande.

The Tewa clowns or Paiakyamû may take part in any Kachina dance but they are confined to the pueblos of the east mesa, especially Hano, where Tewan clans predominate.

Another class of Hopi clowns also of exotic derivation are the Koyimsi[16] which, as the name implies, were derived from Zuñi. Although they may perform in Walpi, their home is in Sichomovi where those clans lived that came from Zuñi.

The order of clowns called the Koyimsi do not paint bands of pigment on their limbs and bodies nor do they, like the Hano clowns, have horns on their heads, but they smear their bodies with earth and wear closely fitted gunnysacks on their heads.

These head coverings have knoblike wens which impart a most ludicrous appearance to the wearers. Their mouths and eyes are made hideous with sausagelike enlargements and they sometimes have similar pendants from above the ears. Their function is not unlike that of the Hano clowns; they amuse spectators during the sacred or Kachina dances. This is an old priesthood, but it has lost that sacred character so marked in the pueblos from which it was derived, and has no altar or fetishes.

The third order of Hopi clowns is limited at the east mesa to Walpi, where it is one of the most important priesthoods, as may be seen by consulting my account of the "New Fire Ceremony," in a previous number of the *Anthropologist*.[17] This is called the Tatcükti or Tataukyamû and the members wear no horns nor helmets on their heads but paint phallic emblems on their backs, breasts, and sometimes on their thighs. They decorate their faces with red bands extending from mouth and eyes to the back of the head, and wear cottontail rabbit tails in their ears, and necklaces of the same around their necks, symbolic of the Rabbit clan that introduced them into Awatobi from the region of the Little Colorado ruins.

This order of clowns has an altar and *tiponi* or palladium, and many traditional songs, and prayers; their acts indicate a form of phallicism in which the obscene is prominent.

The phallic character of their dance dates back to their life in Awatobi from which ruin was obtained a food bowl now in Berlin, which has the dance of the Tataukyamû painted upon it. I possess a photograph of this bowl which represents a number of these priests, wholly naked, dancing in a circle near which is a figure of a woman and another priest. This figure, so far as known, is the earliest known representation of the Tataukyamû dance and the only surviving picture of an Awatobi dance. The same dance is still performed every November at Walpi, but in a modified form, although phallic emblems and elements are conspicuous in the modern survivals.

The first two orders of clowns introduce in the public dances certain droll plays, often obscene, that they invent to amuse the spectators. These drolleries vary with the inventive power of those men who are chosen to take the parts of clowns, and are not ancient. The following episode occurred in one of the dances and was an impromptu exhibition of the Hopi clowns which may have a historical interest, and certainly illustrates the sense of humor of the Hopi Indians. In 1891 the author was engaged in pioneer work with the phonograph in the preservation of Hopi melodies.[18] The use of this instrument naturally made a strong impression on the Hopi who were at first much astonished but later this feeling gave way to amusement when a Graphophone was introduced by the late T. V. Keam.

The value of this instrument for amusement did not escape the clowns, who in one of their performances improvised a phonograph out of an old Sibley stove funnel. Their representation of it is shown in a photograph made by Major Williams in 1892. The bearded person represents the author while the man at the right is one of the clowns. Another clown, hidden under a blanket, responded in a quaking voice to a second performer who from time to time spoke or sang into the funnel, the record being taken down by the bearded Hopi dressed as a white man. The fun thus produced was highly appreciated by the people on the house tops.

### CONCLUSION

The outcome of the above studies of the butterfly cult is that it was introduced by certain Tewan clans which have exerted an influence on the Hopi ritual. We know that many mythological conceptions of ancient date among the Indians can be traced to the Rio Grande region. Take for instance the symbolism of the pottery found in ruins like Sikyatki, Awatobi, or Old Shumopavi. Here we find figures representing Keres and Tewa mythological beings. For instance the symbolic conception of the winged-serpent,[19] as it appears in the winter solstice ceremony at Hano, is thoroughly Tewan and quite different from that at Hopi. Images of that being made of clay on the Tewa Hano altar are different from the effigies used at Walpi. The Hano image has a row of feathers along the back, its eyes, necklace, and teeth, being made of kernels of corn. This horned effigy differs considerably in symbolism from the horned plumed serpent of the southern Hopi clans called Balulukon which is dominant at Walpi. If, however, we compare the Hano clay idol of the feathered horned serpent with the picture on a prehistoric food bowl found at Sikyatki we discover the same row of feathers along the back in both instances. In other words the representation of the Tewa plumed serpent is closer to that of Sikyatki than to that of Walpi, for the latter came from southern Arizona and northern Chihuahua while the Hano was derived directly from the eastern pueblos. This does not necessarily mean that the Hano people came from the same pueblo as the Kokop, but from the same culture area. The Sikyatki people were from Jemez, the Hano from Tcewadi, a ruin on the Rio Grande the site of which is known.

It is interesting in this connection to note that a head similar to the Sikyatki picture of the Plumed Serpent has been found by me at Awatobi showing that the Awatobian had a conception of this mythological being like that of the Sikyatki people. It is anticipated that when the pictures of the Rio Grande plumed serpents have been thoroughly studied they will support the legend that the Sikyatki and Awatobi people came from that region.

It is pointed out in the preceding pages that there still survives a butterfly cult in the Hopi pueblo, Sichomovi, and that it was brought there from the eastern pueblo region, via Zuñi, where for aught I know it still exists. But the cult came originally from the Rio Grande valley and is of Tewa extraction. Facts are presented as evidence supporting the claim that this element of culture is more modern at Hopi than that of the eastern pueblo region. Evidences have been advanced in former publications that considerable additions have been made to the Hopi sociology, linguistics, mythologies, and rites by colonists from the Gila and Salt River valleys, the people that in prehistoric times built the large compounds[20] in southern Arizona. These facts all look one way, viz—the Hopi pueblos as such are comparatively modern in their present settlements. It is evident, as a corollary to the belief that the Hopi culture is more modern than the cultures of the Rio Grande and Gila valleys, that the Hopi language has arisen in comparatively recent times being younger than Keresan, Tewan, or Piman.

PART 8

## INTRODUCTION

Haury's excellent broad survey of Southwestern-Mesoamerican relations was originally published in 1945 in the *Southwestern Journal of Anthropology*, vol. 1, no. 1, pp. 55–74. It marked the beginning of the end of a short period in Southwestern archaeological research during which the dependence of Southwestern cultural developments on those occurring earlier in Mesoamerica had largely been denied by concerned archaeologists. It was not until the renewal of archaeological research in northern Mexico following the end of World War II, coupled with intensive new research in the Southwest itself, that the full impact of Haury's article was felt. As a general survey of the problem, the paper is as valid today as it was on the date of its original publication and remains perhaps the single best work published on the subject. The "elementary conclusions" which he proposes in this article, hypothesizes that the Mesoamerican elements concerned did not all reach the north at the same time. Haury postulates that they moved over not one but several routes, and that they came from various Mesoamerican sources. These conclusions are still completely tenable.

Fieldwork completed or published since 1945 has added an enormous new body of data concerning the problem of Mesoamerican-Southwestern relations. Thus, we now know that a Paleo-Indian-Desert culture base underlies the cultures of Mesoamerica just as in the American Southwest—a question that concerned Haury. Again, the evidence available led Haury to believe that Mesoamerican influence on the Anasazi was nominal and that it came largely through a Hohokam filter; present evidence indicates that Mesoamerican influence on the Anasazi was both much greater and more direct than Haury then believed. Haury, of course, could not anticipate the revelations of the intensive excavations carried out by Charles DiPeso at Casas Grandes in Chihuahua, nor those resulting from his own reexcavations of Snaketown. It can be assumed that Haury now sees even greater influence in Mesoamerica on the Hohokam itself than visualized in this paper.

Haury's discussion of the cultural mechanisms and the geographic routes involved in the Mesoamerican penetration of the

Southwest likewise is still completely valid. Present-day knowledge would place greater emphasis on the position of organized Meso-american trade groups (*pochteca*-like groups) in the relationship; and at least "small group" migration of Mesoamericans into the Southwest now seems possible if not probable. Here, as elsewhere in the paper, all that Haury wrote was tenable in 1945 and generally holds true today. The new data have somewhat shifted the points of emphasis of his arguments, and greatly amplified the weight of many of his tentative conclusions. Haury's paper continues to be the basic source for students of Mesoamerican-Southwestern rela-tions and, as such, is republished in the present volume.

# 12

# THE PROBLEM OF CONTACTS BETWEEN THE SOUTHWESTERN UNITED STATES AND MEXICO

## Emil W. Haury

The problem of relationship between the people of the Southwestern United States and Mexico presents two related aspects: the one, ethnographic; the other, archaeologic. Considerably more has been done with the former in the nature of systematic and theoretical discussions than with the latter.

Beals's excellent paper and subsequent reflections[1] and Kroeber's analysis[2] have impressively set the pace. On the archaeological side, however, the lack of documentation per se and the desultory nature of the studies until very recently have offered few data to stimulate much productive thought. Vaillant's paper[3] dealing with ceramic resemblances of Central and North America is perhaps the only extended venture in the archaeological field. Yet the question of relationship is no less important today than it was then to reach an understanding of the more strictly local problems in the respective areas.

It is not the intent of this paper to present a complete analysis of the resemblances between the areas of high culture developed in Mexico and the Southwest. The chief purpose is to examine briefly a few of the angles and to draw certain inferences. If these prove to be of a controversial nature and as a consequence promote further discussion, or better still, if some fresh archaeological work should be undertaken with the intention of shedding light on this knotty problem, my purpose will have been served.

Many American archaeologists have come to accept as a matter of course the doctrine that many Southwestern culture elements were derived from Mexico. The extreme view has been that Southwestern cultures were little more than marginal and thrice removed radiations from southern centers. These ideas were advanced at a time when the chronologies, and even the patterns of culture, of the respective areas were imperfectly known, all of which made the equation of horizons most difficult. The development of tree-ring dating as a means of adjusting the Southwestern sequences to absolute time and Gila Pueblo's excavations at Snaketown, throwing much new light on the Hohokam culture, caused Gladwin to revolt against what he called "dogma," and to reorient his whole point of view, expressed in volume two of the Snaketown report.[4] This skepticism on his part has had its good effect inasmuch as current workers are exploring the various possibilities much more critically than before. Contrary to my own early leanings somewhat in line with those of Mr. Gladwin, I have reverted to the original premise that the main flow of culture elements was from south to north, beginning with such basic factors as agriculture and pottery. I am willing to concede, however, that house building was so generic a feature and so environmentally determined that its evolution was largely local (as can be shown) after the introduction of the pit house, probably from the Old World. Adherence to the view expressed above does not mean that local peoples were poorly disguised groups of southern tribes or that there was wholesale emigration from Mexico. The Southwestern agricultural peoples should be viewed as having had roots in the demonstrably older preagricultural horizons of the Southwest, so far unmatched by any evidence from central Mexico, and who, when the time came, benefited, to a greater or lesser degree, by transmissions from the fast developing southern centers.

The traits which I believe to be traceable to Mexico were borne by all methods of cultural transmission, from the diffusion of ideas from group to group to the importation of actual objects probably by traders. The weakness in the problem has been our lack of knowledge of northern and especially northwestern Mexico, the terra incognita and the way out of many an archaeologist's dilemma. But even this area is gradually assuming its proper place in the complex history of early America. The growing body of literature, while accounting for some things which are there, also is giving us some indication of what is not there. The works of Sauer and Brand,[5] Sayles,[6] Kelly,[7] Ekholm,[8] and others have lead to the single conclusion that northwestern Mexico was not the main corridor through which the Mexican elements passed to infect the Southwestern cultures. But some sort of relationship did exist and whether this was through the lowlands of the coast or through the sierras remains to be determined. One wonders whether we are not looking for the perfect situation where the diffusion is traceable step by step, whereas a continuous diffusion, without break, need not necessarily have been the case at all.

Few will deny that Mexico and the lands to the south were initially peopled by southward drifting populations. But so far, Mexico has produced practically no evidence of the Paleo-Indian comparable to the patterns of Texas,[9] the Cochise culture,[10] and the San Dieguito[11] complex, known now only north of the international line. This is not because they are absent to the south but because no consistent search has been made for them. The evidence of marine shells from the Gulf of California in the late Pleistocene or early Recent layer in Ventana Cave, associated with a San Dieguito-Folsom complex is a good indication of the potential value of the West Coast in this type of study. Chihuahua, with numerous inland basins, affords excellent chances for the recovery of early remains[12] and it is difficult to imagine that farther south the country is to be found lacking in such evidence. All of this may not be pertinent to the problem but I cannot pass over the subject without lamenting the gross neglect of a challenging field of American archaeology.

So far the evidence of contact is limited to the corn-growing peoples of both areas concerned, and the picture is complicated by the division and subdivision of the cultures. In the Southwest the single large, more or less homogeneous archaeological culture formerly assigned to the whole area has been broken down into at least three basic patterns, the Anasazi, the Hohokam, and the Mogollon, with a fourth, the Patayan, still little more than a suggestion. Each of these displays a complex set of relationships to the other. The role of Mexico must therefore be viewed from the standpoint of each of these and not from all collectively. In the all-important factor of calculating time, the Southwest has the edge over Mexico because of the successful application of tree-ring dating. But this should not cloud the issue by implying that Mexican cultures did not have antiquity or that high or higher planes of existence were not reached there earlier than in the Southwest. That this was so is self-evident, I think, from the nature of the evidence.

The three basic Southwestern archaeologic cultures in which we may look for analogies with Mexico, as stated before, are the Anasazi, Mogollon, and the Hohokam. Geographically, the Anasazi, centering in northwestern New Mexico and northern Arizona, was farthest removed. Beyond the fundamentals of culture, as agriculture, pottery, and loom-weaving with cotton, little of southern origin need be sought there although other isolated and less basic elements might be mentioned, as, for example, a few actual cases of importation.[13] The Mogollon culture, centering in southwestern New Mexico and southeastern Arizona, while in a strategic position to receive impulses from Mexico, had lost its identity everywhere by about A.D. 800, or before many of the specific and definitive southern elements appear in the Southwest. Here, too, only the most basic factors are involved. This leaves the Hohokam of southern Arizona to carry the brunt of any comparison and it was among them that evidence for contact is most concrete. To state this in another way, specific identities with Mexico lie mostly south of the Colorado Plateau, whereas northward the elements are of a more general nature. The few and isolated parallels among the Anasazi, as copper bells, ball courts, the fragment of mosaic mirror with cloisonné at Pueblo Bonito[14] were probably transmitted by the Hohokam and need not imply direct Mexican connections.

The standard approach to a problem such as this is to bring together comparable elements. This is an absorbing game but does not always lead one to the right conclusions. Both Vaillant[15] and Gladwin[16] have noted a number of these, realizing that the meaning is limited.

In the following list, supplemented graphically by figures *1* and *2*, some additional parallels are given. Let me stress again that no effort has been made to canvass the situation completely but merely to present enough of the general picture to guide to conclusions stated presently. The elements are divided into two categories on the basis of their general effect on the receptor groups: (1) the primary and fundamental elements which definitely lifted the plane of culture; and (2) the secondary elements which, while distinctive, added little more than frills to the culture of the receptor group.

**Primary Elements**

Corn and corn culture:[17] to Hohokam, Mogollon, and Anasazi by about A.D. 1.

Pottery: first to Hohokam and Mogollon, by about A.D. 1, whence the germ spread (by about 400) to the Anasazi.

Cotton and (inferentially) the loom: first to the Hohokam (probably before 700) and quickly transmitted to the Anasazi by them.

Concept of Stone carving in relief in the full-round: primarily to Hohokam before 700, and restricted by them to carving miniatures, never for architectural decoration.[18] Rare among other groups.

**Secondary Elements**

Ball courts: to Hohokam by about 800[19] and via the Hohokam to the Anasazi (Flagstaff area), by about 1050.[20]

Copper bells: to Hohokam and Anasazi, by about 1100.[21]

Macaw: chiefly to Anasazi, by 1100.[22]

**Pottery Traits**

Footed vessels: to Hohokam, before 700 (fig. *1*, a, b).[23]

Legged vessels: to Hohokam, by 700 (fig. *1*, c, d).

Handled censer: to Hohokam, by about 500 (fig. *1*, e, f).

Bossed decoration: to Hohokam, by 700, and via Hohokam to Anasazi (fig. *1*, g, h, i).

Candeleros: to Hohokam, by 500 (?) (fig. *1*, j, k).

Effigy vessels: to Hohokam, by 300 (?) (fig. *1*, l, m).

Baking griddles: to Hohokam, by 1200.[24]

Pictorial elements:[25] to Anasazi (Mimbres), by about 1150 (fig. *1*, n, o).

### Other Clay Objects

Figurines: to Hohokam, Mogollon and Anasazi, early centuries of the Christian era, probably as an associate of pottery (fig. *2*, a–e).

Spindle whorls: mainly to Hohokam, by about 1200 (fig. *2*, f–l).

### Stone Elements

Spool-shaped ear plugs: to Hohokam, by 1000 (fig. *2*, m, n).[26]

Nose plugs: to Hohokam, by 1000 (fig. *2*, o–q).

Mosaic discs (with iron pyrites overlay): to Hohokam before 700, and with pseudo-cloisonné decoration somewhat later.[27]

Chak Mool-like figure: to Hohokam, by 500 (fig. 2, r).

Chipped crescents: to Hohokam, by 1000 (fig. *2*, s, t).

Mano with overhanging ends: to Hohokam (Desert Branch), by 1300[28] (fig. *2*, u, v).

Cross-shaped stones: to north Mexican and southern Arizona peoples by about 1000 (fig. *2*, w, x).

Shaped mortars: to Hohokam, by 800 (fig. *2*, y, z).

Figurine with vessel on head: to Hohokam, by about 1000 (fig. *2*, aa–bb).

### Textile Techniques

Gauze weave: to Hohokam, by 1100, and via Hohokam to Anasazi.[29]

Weft-wrap openwork: to Hohokam and Anasazi, by 1100.[30]

Tie-dying (?): evidence so far is limited to Anasazi of 1200 or later.

The status of canal irrigation, cremation, throwing clubs, atlatls (spear-throwers), fur robes, and three-quarter grooved axes is debatable. The last named is early in the Hohokam culture[31] and may have spread south as its distribution is pretty well limited to northern Mexico. Fur robes, throwing clubs, and the atlatl were widespread on an early plane and may have gone in either direction. Evidence for cremation is perhaps older in the Southwest than in Mexico and opportunities for the development of canal irrigation would appear to have been better in the arid Southwest than elsewhere.

If the parallels listed are accepted as having had southern origins we arrive at the following elementary conclusions: (1) that the elements did not all move north at the same time, but began to spread as early as the dawn of the Christian era, continuing up into historic times; (2) that they did not all travel over the same route, some having reached the Southwestern frontiers over a northwesterly lowland course, while others appear to have moved through the highlands to the east; and (3) that all did not come from the same source.[32] Some are distinctly Middle American in flavor, others are matched most closely by traits in the Mexican highland cultures, and a few are from the northern fringes of the high cultures of Mexico.

This means that we should not look for a fixed route of entry, pointing back to a single culture group, or that we should endeavor to find traces of a band of people which emigrated wholesale from Mexico. The Mexican accretions were strongest in the Hohokam culture about A.D. 700 and 1100, which in itself suggests infiltration by the normal processes of diffusion. Actual contact by southern traders undoubtedly existed but their influence was largely limited to the goods they carried.

The overall picture is one in which the Southwestern groups (particularly the Hohokam and Mogollon), with roots in preceramic and preagricultural levels of culture, received the stimulus of higher attainments from the outside, and in this case from the south. This has become evident from the result of work in recent years with respect to the Cochise culture and its probable connections with the Hohokam and Mogollon, and more particularly has this been brought out by the findings in Ventana Cave where the transition from a preagricultural and preceramic status to agriculture and pottery was made without an apparent upheaval of people. This case shows logically that the Hohokam were descendants of the earlier food-gathering hunting folk.[33]

This brings us now to speculation as to the routes of entry and as to possible linked traits. Efforts to establish a corridor through Sonora and Sinaloa have been largely negative.[34] It has been suggested that such an avenue must lie farther to the east, toward or in the Sierra Madres. This may very well have been the case, but I believe there is some evidence to support the contention that an early wave of influence passed through the northwestern Mexican states. The best indication is botanical in nature. Beals shows[35] a continuous band of maize agriculture up the West Coast (the most desolate section excepted) and extending into southern Arizona. In far western Arizona, agriculture was present, too, but not of primary importance. The type of corn grown through the lower Colorado River basin by the Yuman peoples and also by the Piman peoples north of the international line to the Gila Valley is a hot country corn, Anderson and Cutler's "Pima-Papago" race of Zea Mays, in contrast to the "Pueblo" race of the Plateau.[36] Significantly, Pima-Papago corn is the ancient type of the area, too, grown by the Hohokam and preserved in Ventana Cave.[37] Equally meaningful is the fact that Pima-Papago corn is quite similar to Basketmaker corn.[38] It looks as though both the

Hohokam and the Basketmakers received a corn, probably by A.D. 1, suited to an arid environment on the initial northward diffusion of this all-important cereal, and that the Basketmakers were able to adapt it to a somewhat higher and cooler climate. Subsequent accretions, but not through the northwest Mexican or southern Arizona territories, lead to the development of the Pueblo race of corn. It is likely, too, that the Mogollon culture, with southern frontiers in northeastern Sonora and northern Chihuahua, received corn at about the same time.[39]

With corn cultivation, or directly on the heels of its northward expansion, I believe we can postulate the arrival of pottery. This reached the Hohokam and Mogollon first[40] and the germ spread somewhat later to the Basketmaker who then went through most of the developmental stages under their own initiative. It is clear that early Mogollon and Hohokam pottery becomes more alike as one inspects older and older material. This refers to color, range of types, and design. The assumption of a common parentage for the pottery of these two groups is quite in line with the evidence. Further, what I consider of importance is the similarity of this earliest Southwestern ceramic fabric to the polished red, polished black, brown ware, and broad line red-painted types of the Middle Cultures of the Mexican highlands. The earliest manifestations of the Middle Cultures, believed to date before the time of Christ,[41] show a higher plane of development than do the oldest remains we now have for the Hohokam and the Mogollon. I see no probability that pottery will prove to be earlier than A.D. 1 in the Southwest.

A third element which may have been connected with this first period of expansion is the clay figurine. There is no use denying that many unrelated peoples have made figurines and that similarities among them did occur. But here we are dealing with complexes in contiguous areas, as well as with some rather specific analogies, thereby reducing the possibility of coincidence. Figurines were known in the Hohokam from the time they had pottery.[42] We also have evidence now that the Mogollon culture was acquainted with figurines by the fourth century.[43] A simple slab-type of figurine is also found in the Basketmaker III,[44] possibly a far northern extension of the idea. The general similarity in style among these is shown in figure 2, a–e. It needs to be pointed out, however, that the examples illustrated from Cuicuilco are not in the normal style for the site. They may well be survivals of a style from which the Southwestern forms were drawn, a style representative of an horizon of the Middle Cultures of Mexico which needs still to be determined.

The scheme just outlined—the recognition of a radiation of elements by about A.D. 1—agrees in the main with Ekholm,[45] who has worked at the problem from the southern or Mexican end. He also discerns a period of later contacts, a thesis with which I am in full agreement. This was after A.D. 500, with a probable peak of contact reached at about 1000. The Southwestern group affected was chiefly the Hohokam. The list already given demonstrates well enough the character and the approximate time of the elements involved.

There is no direct evidence to show over what route these traveled. Since resemblances occur in greater number among the River Hohokam, we may guess that the corridor lay well to the west in northwestern Mexico, either through Sinaloa and Sonora over routes similar to those followed by the early Spaniards, or somewhat farther to the east along the western foothills of the Sierras. Here the river systems generally trend north and south, their heads leading directly to the upper drainages of the Santa Cruz and San Pedro rivers, feeder of the Gila and the homeland of the Hohokam. Connections with Durango, the northern outpost of high cultures of Mexico would not appear too difficult to establish. It is worth noting that excavations in the states of Sonora and Sinaloa to date have all been in late horizons, too late to pick up many of the elements involved in this discussion, if the corridor was coastal.

That contacts were established between the Hohokam and northwestern Mexico in a late prehistoric time level can be shown. Excavations by the Arizona State Museum in Papagueria have focused attention on several elements which, beyond question, were immediately derived from Sinaloan sources. These are spindle whorls[46] (fig. 2, f, h), the strange and highly characteristic mano with overhanging ends (fig. 2, u, v), tortilla slabs[47] or griddles, and probably a short effigy pestle. In addition the marked resemblance in the red ware between Sinaloa and Papagueria has also been noted.[48] These elements all appear late in the Hohokam area, after 1200. The earlier connections with the south, possibly over a more easterly route, had ceased to exist by this time when the Hohokam culture was ebbing.

Information is also accumulating to bring the Trincheras culture into adjustment with the Hohokam sequence. This is worth mentioning here because we shall go much farther in the correlations if relationship is established between adjoining groups rather than by making large aerial jumps. Brand[49] has called attention to the fact that the international boundary marks the line of separation between the Trincheras and the southern limits of what we know as Hohokam. This coincides with our observations, too, and for a while it appeared as though there were little exchange between the two. Trincheras wares are now appearing with regularity in sites north of the border[50] and the association is with Colonial and Sedentary period remains. Conversely, Hohokam elements have been recognized in the large and significant site at La Playa.[51] In fact, the similarity in the fundamental characters of the Trincheras culture and that of the Desert Hohokam of Papagueria urgently calls for a revision of our concept of Hohokam, a need which Kroeber has already pointed out,[52] based on larger considerations.

In Chihuahua, the situation is somewhat better understood. On a probable Mogollon basis,[53] Chihuahua culture was later strongly influenced from the Southwest,[54] first from the Mimbres area and swayed still later by the southwardly expanding Salado. Southern Mexican ceramic derivations at this time appear to have been a form of black-on-red pottery according to Sayles,[55] and Ekholm[56] sees resemblances between the effigy vessels of Chihuahua and those of the Tarascan area.

It will be quite evident to the critical reader that the arguments presented herein and the nature of the data on which they are based fall short of being convincing. This is due basically to the inadequacy of the information which, so far, is in inverse proportion to the weight of the problem.

The parallels mentioned have been drawn chiefly from central Mexico, involving a jump of over a thousand miles and an almost complete disregard of the intervening area. This omission is forced on us because the archaeological story of northwestern Mexico has not yet been written. When culture patterns and sequences have been determined for that vast region, the distribution of the traits which seem important in linking the Southwest and the high cultures of Mexico may prove to be more continuous than is evident now, thereby strengthening the present thesis. They may, however, be lacking as the result of discontinuous diffusion. Further excavation alone can elucidate this aspect of the problem.

Beyond this necessity, something may be done toward setting the stage for a sounder approach to the problem by a reorientation of our thinking with respect to the southern limit of the Southwest as a culture area. This has never been satisfactorily set up, although, on the strength of ethnological data and, by inference, on archaeological evidence, too, Beals[57] has argued forcefully that this limit might be carried south to include the Cora and Huichol in Nayarit and Jalisco and that some such term as the "Greater Southwest" be used to encompass both the American and Mexican sectors. In Beals's words, "the problem of relations between northern Mexico and the Southwest" would then become "the problem of accounting for differentiation within the Greater Southwest." Obviously, this would not make the task of solving the problems easier, but with the Southwestern cultural frontier much nearer the high centers of develop-

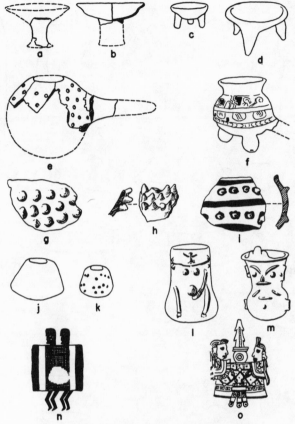

FIG. 1. Southwestern and Mexican archaeological objects.

ment on the Mexican Plateau than it is at present, the forging of the final links would appear much less difficult.

Another step, calculated to consolidate existing archaeological evidence, would be the reexamination of acknowledged cultural frameworks in the Southwest, as the Hohokam and Mogollon, with the idea of relating to them cultural manifestations which at the moment are dangling. The incorporation of Trincheras with Hohokam has already been mentioned as desirable. Others, too, as the pattern south of the Sonora River and still another on the Mayo River,[58] might be brought into the Southwestern scheme with little added work. This would at least have the salutary effect of progressing from the known to the unknown, the only rational and safe approach to the problem of pre-Columbia Mexican-Southwestern contacts.

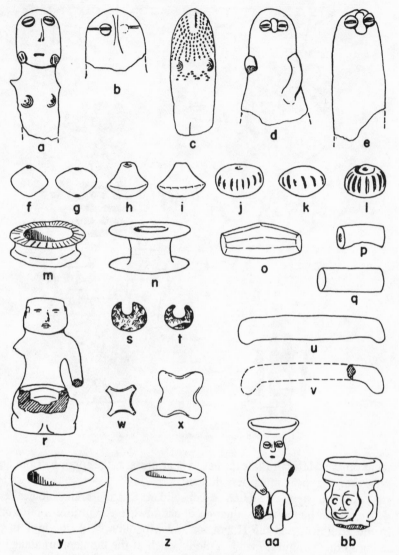

FIG. 2. Southwestern and Mexican archaeological objects.

*PART 9*

# INTRODUCTION

A. L. Kroeber in this sweeping paper published in 1928 discusses not only the Southwest but the similarities and differences of Southwestern culture to that of Mexico, California, the Northwest Coast, the Plains, and the Southeast. He especially emphasizes the implications for contact within these various regions. The paper is rich in detail and in inference. It was inspired largely by the publication of Strong's paper on Southwestern society the preceding year (reproduced in a previous volume of this series)[1] and by the development of the "Pecos Chronology" later in 1927. Some of the gaps in our knowledge of native cultures have since been filled. For example, our picture of central Mexico is now rich and detailed and the bemoaned lacunae of data for northern Mexico is finally being filled. In terms of the Southeast, however, though the terminology has changed and dates are firmer, there is no great advance from Kroeber's day to the present in understanding the movement of culture items and peoples.

In this paper, Kroeber first clearly expressed a number of ideas that were to receive considerable attention from anthropologists in later years. Here we find the first definitive statement of the concept of the "Greater Southwest" as both a cultural and ecological area, and its division into two parallel cultural traditions and areas: the Pueblo [Anasazi] and the Gila-Sonoran [Hohokam]. He recognized the essential similarity of the red-on-buff ceramics found in Arizona, Sonora, and southern California, and commented on the significance of their survival in the cultures of the contemporary Pima, Papago, Mohave, and Maricopa ethnic groups. He further suggested the probable intrusion of this ceramic tradition into the Southwest from an outside source, presumably Mesoamerica. Puebloan culture, he specifically identifies as a local development out of a basic "Basketmaker" cultural horizon (today conceptualized as the Southwestern Archaic, or broadly speaking, the Desert culture) combined with Mexican elements. In comparing Pueblo and Navaho cultures and their ecological matrix, he very nearly anticipated Redfield's conceptualization of "Great and Little Traditions" by nearly three decades. Finally, in view of a still raging controversy, it should be noted that Kroeber considers with approval the possibility that two traits of mutative Polynesian cultural origins have become incorporated in the cultures of southern California!

As an overview, Kroeber's summation of the salient features of a large segment of American Indian culture is still valid today, and a number of the concepts which he developed in this paper anticipated by many years their general acceptance in the field of anthropology.

# 13

# NATIVE CULTURE OF THE SOUTHWEST

## A. L. Kroeber

Anthropology has been pursued in the Southwest for a couple of generations. The railroad surveys and early geological explorations brought back descriptions, specimens, and photographs, both of ruins and pueblos, some of which have never been surpassed. Excavations soon followed, and in some cases work was done which will stand for all time: Mindeleff's on architecture, for instance. Meanwhile Cushing laid the foundation of ethnological study in his residence at Zuñi. Materials kept piling up decade by decade.

Fifteen to twenty years ago inquiries took a new turn. The older investigators had been content to describe or, if they explained, felt confident that they could derive origins immediately from their particular data. In time, objectives shifted from origins to development, from ultimate to nearer antecedents, and even these, it was recognized, could ordinarily be determined only through comparative treatment of a wide body of data. In archaeology the tremendous evidential weight of superimposition of remains began to be perceived, and with the stratigraphic discoveries of Nelson and Kidder[1] Southwestern archaeology entered the field of the modern sciences. Site after site was explored under the new point of view; until, basing on the long continued excavations at Pecos, Kidder, in his *Southwestern Archaeology*,[2] was able to weld the prehistory of the most distinctive part of the area into a comprehensive and continuous whole of two Basketmaker and five Pueblo periods. This fundamental work will no doubt be corrected in detail, enriched and intensified, and certainly is in need of areal extension; but its framework promises to be permanent.

Ethnology has not progressed quite so far, but is emerging from the descriptive stage. When Parsons's long promised monograph appears, we shall have an analytic comparison and partial historic interpretation of at least the important ritual side of Southwestern culture; and studies of its other aspects may be expected to follow. Strong has already made a beginning of an interpretation for the forms of society.[3]

It is opportune, accordingly, to review the problems of cultural anthropology in the native Southwest as they shape themselves at present.

First of all, it must be admitted that we recognize several different Southwests. The archaeologists mean Pueblo and the agricultural antecessors of the Pueblo, when they say Southwest. Ethnologists mostly have in mind Pueblo and Navaho, with the Pima-Papago as a sort of annex. The Apache are little known; the Havasupai remain undescribed in print;[4] on Walapai, Yavapai, Maricopa, there is nothing. Haeberlin long ago did not hesitate to treat the southern Californians as outright Southwestern,[5] but in most discussions they are still left out, as if they were ethnically Californian. Wissler[6] and I,[7] in continental classifications, both extend the Southwest culture south nearly to the Tropic, so that half of it lies in Mexico. No one appears to have challenged this classification, perhaps because data from northern Mexico are so scant. At the same time, it is clear that if this larger Southwest is a true cultural entity, the old Pueblo or even Arizona-New Mexico Southwest is but a fragment, whose functioning is intelligible only in terms of the larger growth. What is the common element in all the tribal cultures of the area? What is the substratum from which they have developed divergently, and what are the interrelations between the developments? Considerations of this sort are perhaps being faced in many quarters. They have not yet been attacked as problems.

What is needed first of all is a more intensive comprehension of the area as a setting; of the human ecology of the native Southwest. Wissler has pointed out that the modern Pueblo region falls wholly within a region which geographical botanists describe as a semidesert bordering on plains, forest, and desert.[8] For the remainder of the Southwest even such preliminary correlation has scarcely been attempted.

Maps of botanical distribution, however, show as a well defined area of desert, characterized by creosote bush and cactaceae, the territory occupied by almost the whole Yuman family and the Pima, Papago, and Sonoran tribes, in other words, those Southwestern peoples who might be described as sub-Pueblo. On the other hand, the semidesert in which the Pueblo range falls, extends northwestward into the Great Basin. This fact, at first sight seemingly subversive of a correlation between Pueblo culture and environment, nevertheless accords with the extension into Nevada of a form of the Basketmaker culture of which the Pueblo was an outgrowth.

In this matter of ecology it is of course not enough to know that an area is arid and that the agricultural natives evinced skill in finding water holes or spots in which their corn would grow. The local variations of season, temperature, precipitation, physiography, soil, plant cover, and dependent fauna mean an inevitable adjustment of the local cultures. We have unduly neglected ecology in almost all North American ethnological studies. Attention has been directed to cultural forms; the land, and those aspects of culture most directly dependent on it, economics and politics, have been slighted. They lend themselves less readily to systematization than society, ritual, tradition, and art, and their patterns are hence more plastic and harder to follow. But they are no less significant to the understanding of culture processes, and the Southwest, a land that is open and boldly characterized, offers particular opportunity for a modern, non-simplistic environmental study, which would almost certainly stimulate analogous research elsewhere. What seems to be most needed at the outset is a review and ordering of the geographical data available.

The historic imports of the spatial relations of the various culture types in the Southwest have been little examined except in so far as Kidder has dealt with the southward retraction of the true Pueblo area in its third or Great period,[9] its abandonment of its original focus, the San Juan drainage, at the end of that period, and its gradual northward and eastward shrinkage since. Equally interesting are likely to be inductions based on the space and time distribution of traits transcending the special Pueblo culture: pottery, for instance.

Except perhaps for some of the Athabascans and Yumans, every Southwestern people seems to have been pottery making. To the west of the trichrome and glazing art of the Pueblos, pottery becomes two-color on the lower Gila and Colorado, monochrome in California. This indicates a relation of marginal dependence on the Pueblo art. But a direct dependence of these peripheral areas on the Pueblo center is not borne out by other considerations. The middle ("lower") Gila region has to date shown two styles of pottery, recognized but misinterpreted many years ago by Cushing:[10] a red-white-black, and a two-color called variously red-on-yellow, red-on-gray, red-on-red, or, most appropriately, red-on-buff. This bichrome ware is, as Kidder has pointed out,[11] "so radically unlike . . . all other Southwestern (read Pueblo) pottery that it gives rise to the suspicion that it may be the result of an intrusion from some hitherto unlocated culture centre." As to the distinctness of this ware in texture, color, pattern, and probably shape, there can be no question; although the small-element designs figured by Kidder represent only one strain in the style. There can also be no question as to the essential survival of this style in the pottery art of the recent Colorado River tribes, the Yuma and Mohave; and beyond them, in a simplified, usually patternless stage, among the southern California groups. Mohave pottery is almost identical with ancient middle Gila red-on-buff ware in texture and color; even the designs, although of a somewhat new cast, show indubitable relationship. Modern Pima and Maricopa ware would seem to represent a somewhat more altered making-over of the same tradition, with the substitution of black vegetable paint for the dull red in the designs. From Fresnal, in southern Arizona, Lumholtz[12] has figured two ancient bowls closely similar to the red-on-buff of the Gila. Seri pottery, according to McGee's description and illustrations,[13] belongs to the same tradition, without more simplification, or more quality of archaic survival, than the ware of southern California. The style thus has a distribution embracing at least northwestern Sonora, southwestern Arizona, southern California, perhaps northern Baja California—an area roughly as large as the Pueblo area at the time of its greatest extension. These two pottery traditions in the main abutted on and excluded each other.

They did however geographically overlap in the middle Gila drainage. Kidder was able to place the Pueblo-like middle Gila trichrome toward the end of the Pueblo Great period (P III),[14] without having the evidence to place red-on-buff temporally. Schmidt, who subsequently excavated in the region, showed by stratification and cross-typing of stray sherds that the red-on-buff is the earlier of the two styles.[15] This brings to the fore the interesting fact that the red-on-buff, although temporarily displaced by a Pueblo style on the Gila, has maintained itself with relatively little change over most of its area at least since early Pueblo III times, whereas during the same period black-on-white went out, glaze developed and decayed, and modern styles arose in the Pueblo area.

This vitality of the red-on-buff style reenforces the inferences drawn from its distinctness and extension. It represents a movement no doubt ultimately related but largely independent of Pueblo pottery growth and approximately equal to it in historical and geographical significance. It is merely the fact that we have approached the ancient contact manifestations of this separate growth from the angle of Pueblo development and hesitated to connect it with its natural survivals, which has obscured the picture. We can accordingly no longer with propriety substantially equate Pueblo and Southwestern in speaking of pottery. Southwestern pottery history consists of at least two developments and their interrelations: Pueblo and Gila-Sonora.

This recognition raises the presumption that Southwestern culture in general is to be viewed in the same way. If we could feel sure of doing so legitimately, the anomalous position of the Pima as a sort of irrelevant appendix would at once be done away with. Just as corrugating, black-on-white, and glazing characterize the pottery of the distinctive Pueblo unit of this larger culture mass, so would storied masonry, community construction, the kiva, cotton, the matrilineate, direction-color symbolism, perhaps priesthood by learning to fill a recognized office, altars, masks, ancestor impersonation, the importance of the ideas of emergence from the underworld and of sex fertilization, characterize Pueblo culture. The Gila-Sonora culture growth is as yet too little known to be equally well definable; but it would seem to lack most or all of the cited Pueblo trends, and to possess instead patrilinear institutions, a fighting tradition and war legends, village as opposed to town organization, prevailingly shamanistic control of ritual, probably irrigation. The environmental reflection of the divergence is that the Pueblo area is semidesert, the Gila-Yuman-Sonoran area true desert.

This view would explain the isolated Casa Grande culture as a transient contact phenomenon of the two major culture growths. It might also go far to clear up the puzzling cultural status of the lower Colorado tribes, who on the one hand are specialized away from what it has been customary to regard as "Southwestern" features, and on the other hand lack a number of traits common to the Pueblos and the littoral groups of southern California: the kiva sweathouse, for instance, group fetishes, initiation ceremonies, sand painting altars, moiety organization. Strong, who recognizes in California older Pueblo and later Colorado River influences,[16] has suggested[17] a migrational irruption of the Yuman tribes to account for the geographical break in recent cultural continuity. It would be less hypothetical to find the explanation in a northward extension of Sonoran culture influences cutting across an earlier westward radiation of Pueblo influences, without commitment as to populational shifts. No doubt the Yuman River tribes specialized considerably the Sonoran culture which reached them. Almost certainly, too, part of the southern culture elements received were passed on by them to the southern Californians—pottery, for example, perhaps the Dying God concept, and the tale of the hero who recovered the bones of his father who had been killed when he lost a game, or whose bones were being played with by his slayers—two myth ideas that it is difficult not to connect with their occurrences in southern Mexico.[18] Such secondary growths and diffusions, however, enrich rather than break the picture which the history of the larger Southwest is beginning to reveal in outline.

Where knowledge is most needed, of course, is on northern Mexico. An intensive modern study of the ethnology of a single Sonoran tribe, for instance, would go far to confirm, modify, or overthrow the views just outlined. To date, the international boundary has proved an almost complete barrier to the broader understanding of the Southwest. And yet the new background, the somewhat diverse technique of field approach, the different language medium, are not great difficulties; certainly not sufficient to warrant continuing to deal with the Southwest as if it consisted essentially of its Pueblo subarea. Certain problems that have already arisen may very likely find a prompt solution as soon as the southern half of the Southwest is taken cognizance of: the apparently local invention of Southwestern pottery in the Basketmaker era, for instance.[19] On general grounds this invention seems improbable, as Morris recognizes. Yet, as long as a Mexican origin means a substantially direct derivation from the well-particularized Archaic of the Valley of Mexico, specialists in the Southwest are sound in preferring to consider an independent origin of pottery in their own area. With nearer Mexican types in their ken, and the possibility of tracing stimuli as well as imitations, they might feel differently.

Unusually interesting is the cultural positions of the Seri, of which McGee's monograph evidently gives a warped or considerably misinterpreted picture. As he saw the Seri, they do not fit into any historic or cultural scheme, but stand apart to a degree unparalleled in North American experience. It is indicated that McGee's work is in need of reviewing on the basis of much fuller evidence. The Seri language, for instance, is not only not isolated, but reasonably similar to Yuman.[20] Their pottery, as already mentioned, seems to have Yuman affinities. There is not a single specific fact in McGee's monograph that compels the acceptance of the Seri as matrilineal and matriarchal; he seems never to have got real evidence as to how they reckoned descent.

The sanest interpretation of the anomalies of the Seri would seem to be that they are a Yuman group that crossed the relatively narrow[21] part of the Gulf of California from the Peninsula to Tiburon island and adjacent tracts which the Sonoran agricultural populations had left waste, but to which they could transfer without much change of their mid-Peninsular culture. In direct contact with more advanced peoples, especially after the Spanish occupation, they became half predatory, half parasitic; perhaps with an accompanying tendency to cultural degeneration. There is at any rate nothing romantic in such a view; and if it has foundation, the analysis of Seri culture will prove extremely interesting.

Recently Loeb has construed the culture of the Pomo of north central California as marginal to that of the Pueblos on the basis of their matrilineal tendencies, meal offerings, ritual pole-climbing, rattlesnake ceremony, spirit impersonations, and shamanistic societies.[22] This seems a slender list of traits for the interpretation of Pomo culture as historically dependent on that of the Pueblos, especially as half of the list is lacking in nearer south central California, among the Yokuts. At the same time a historical connection does seem indicated for at least some of the more specific traits. The nature and route of the transmission may become clear with fuller knowledge of the intervening groups.

Recently also the pottery of south central California has become better known, and proves to extend from the San Joaquin Valley to southern Nevada.[23] In spite of its outward crudity, it is a true pottery, made by coiling. The easterly area which it is now known to have occupied brings it nearly in contact with lower Colorado River pottery. It no longer seems likely, however, that the Virgin-Muddy drainage pottery in Nevada represents a taking over of the art from the Mohave, for the characteristic color and designs of the latter are lacking, and the similarities are with central California, according to the description of M. R. Harrington. At the same time, some relation is almost necessarily to be assumed. It begins to look as if there had been two flows of pottery art westward into California: one from the lower Colorado into the southern part of the state, the other from the area north of the middle Colorado into the central part, the intervening highland tract—Tehachapi to Santa Barbara—accepting neither.

This intervening area shows several other features that interrupt what would otherwise be continuous distributions: absence of moieties, burial instead of cremation, bottleneck basketry.[24] It is not unthinkable that the solitary spear-thrower recorded from California, the Santa Barbara specimen brought home by Vancouver, which is so strikingly aberrant in form,[25] represents a survival somehow connected with what happened in this potteryless tract. The cotton Pueblo cloth, cylinder-headed club, Mohave style hair curls, found at Buena Vista Lake in the San Joaquin-Tulare Valley,[26] seem rather to be the result of a flow or transport northwestward across the area in question. This unique lot of material is likely to remain puzzling for a long time, both because it is unaccompanied by age indications and because its affiliations are heterogeneous as to area and period.

More definite is the rich cave material from north central Nevada being described by Loud and Harrington.[27] This shows general central Californian affinities, but in its lower levels, so far as these were determinable, specific Basketmaker resemblances also: spear-throwers, for instance. Of further importance in this connection are the positive determinations of specific Pueblo culture being made, especially by Harrington, in southern Nevada.[28] These seem to be fairly early, probably Pueblo II. The upshot of these discoveries appears to be that an early connection of California with the northern Southwest through the southern Great

Basin, which has long been suspected for the Basketmaker period, was succeeded, either immediately or after an intermission, by a northwestward raying out of early Pueblo culture at a time when its northwest extension was greater than subsequently. Even the modern pottery of southern Nevada and central California may represent an echo of this Pueblo expansion. Later, as the true Pueblo area contracted, there may have been transient protrusions or proliferations from it, which, coupled with the losses due to transmission into another set of cultural forms, may account for the apparent sporadic nature of Southwestern traits in central California and beyond. From the point of view of the Southwest, we are here at the very borders of its area if not influence, and history is likely to have been tangled. Yet it is already clear that events in the Southwest cannot be disregarded in understanding what happened well within an area reckoned as distinct. This accords with environment: phytogeographically the Basin and the Pueblo portion of the Southwest form part of one major area of semidesert.

Returning to territory that is well within the Southwest, we find Strong[29] describing the southern California Indians—other than those of the Colorado River—as organized into small, land-owning, politically autonomous groups, each constituting a male lineage with a patriarchal head who has in his custody, in his house, a fetish bundle containing the more important ceremonial paraphernalia of the group. This type of society holds among the poorer tribes, such as the Desert Cahuilla. In the more prosperous tribes close to the coast, the small unit groups combined into villages. Gifford[30] has shown that there is considerable warrant for assuming lineages, prevailingly paternal and landowning, as the basis of society in all of California, the larger organizations, such as clans, moieties, villages, and tribes, having been built out of or upon them. In central and northern California, the group is without a fetish bundle; but among the Pueblos the fetish concept reappears with important functions and associated both with houses and with groups. The lineage is also easily traced within the Pueblo clan, although often nameless, and matrilineal. Strong therefore concludes with every appearance of reason that Pueblo and perhaps all Southwestern society in the United States grew out of a status approximately represented by the modern Shoshonean tribes of southern California.

Apparently this growth among the Pueblo has to be pictured as a process of union of lineages into clans and clans into towns; a loss of most of the political autonomy of the lineages, and of territorial propriety except perhaps for farm land-tracts; the elaboration of ritual organization with differentiation of official functions; partial segregation of religious and profane houses; and multiplication of initiating cult societies. Hand in hand went an extension of the fetish concept until not only every group, ritual as well as socially hereditary, but in some cases the individual members of cult societies, possessed their own fetishes. Meanwhile too the lineages had reconstituted themselves on a maternal instead of paternal basis of reckoning descent. This presumably would have happened in connection with the permanent attachment of women to houses, or their coming to own houses, however one prefers to view the relation.

There is nothing in recent Pueblo society to contravene such a resolution of its history, and much to support it. For instance, among the California Shoshoneans initiated members of the cults and shamans are unusually difficult to distinguish. The Pueblo counterpart is that shamanism as such is practically absent, its functions being largely taken over by curing cult societies. It even seems possible to reconstruct conjecturally something of the history of Southwestern ceremonialism by analogy with the southern Californians. Sand painting altars, for instance, should be older than masks or Kachina gods. Other questions would be raised rather than answered. Thus, the problem whether the Pueblo tribal Kachina society or the curing societies are older, would not be specially illuminated by southern California conditions, because the one cult organization there is both concerned with tribal status and shamanistically colored. Nor, in other cases, could an inference be ventured, because of the possibilities of local influencing by a third set of populations. Importance of use of Datura—toloache—for instance, could by no means be construed as having once characterized Pueblo religion as it now characterizes that of southern California. Still, the relation of the two areas does open potentialities of inferring backward in time; if not to ancient Pueblo, then to ancient Sonora.

The coastal Shoshonean organization should therefore match approximately that in vogue in one or more periods of Pueblo archaeology. Basketmaker II or III is at once suggested, possibly Pueblo I—eras of small groups essentially restricting themselves to limited tracts; sedentary in the sense of not roaming widely and of spending part of each year at a site that was home; unsettled, however, in comparison with historic Pueblo town groups. Pueblo I, more likely II, would have been the period of first drawing together of lineages into groups, which, by Pueblo II, the Great period, had consolidated still farther into large pueblos each presumably containing several multiple-lineage clans. In this era of Pueblo II and III there would also have been taking place the shift from patrilineal to matrilineal reckoning: if this was connected with women's house ownership, it may be assumed to have been most likely to occur at a time of marked alteration of house use, and this would have been at the inception of town life, with its relatively stable and large concentrations. There would be no implication that particular lineages continued unbroken through the shift from male to female reckoning. Such a continuance is hard to imagine. With the change of descent, the lineages as such would dissolve into a status of confused or ambiguous definition of the adherence of individuals, from which, perhaps within a couple of generations, new lineages with changed descent would crystallize out, the idea or pattern of grouping by unilateral descent having continued.

These reconstructions may savor too heavily of the hypothetical. If so, it is because they are premature. When based on sufficiently full knowledge, they need not be less sound than other and more familiar historical reconstructions based on inferences. They illustrate the possibility of cooperative relation between the archaeological and ethnological approaches. In the field of intangibles, there is no reason why the archaeologist should refrain from using the distributional inductions of ethnology; nor why the ethnologist should hesitate to buttress his findings as to the history of culture forms and organization by converting, as well as may be, the tangibles actually established by the excavator, into their corresponding intangibles.

In one respect the heart of the American Southwest is unique in North America. This is its possession of two parallel and heavily interinfluencing streams of culture, the agricultural and nonagricultural. These evidently behave toward each other somewhat like classes in a single society. Navaho and Hopi, to be sure, feel toward each other like two adjacent European nationalities of separate cultural tradition. But, also like these, they impart culture material to each other. And the economic base of society is so thoroughly different that a remarkable contrast has become established between the essential uniformity in the formal or upper levels of the two cultures and the diversity in the underlying ones. The Navaho sand-painting altars and meteorological and fertilization symbolism, for instance, must inevitably have been taken over from the agricultural Pueblos, and fitted into an old anarchic, priestless scheme of more or less shamanistic curing ritual, with little other effect than to invest this with vividness and picturesque interest. In fact, freed from the close intent and official tradition of the Pueblos, the painting of the Navaho took on aesthetic quality superior to that of their masters. Navaho myth and legend are similarly filled with Pueblo material, again treated with a freedom which the better defined purposes of the Pueblos did not allow. The matrilineal reckoning of the Navaho, so anomalous in combination with their unsettled life and patrilocal residence, is also almost certainly taken over from the Pueblos; and so with their weaving—a strange art to occur among a people practically without baskets and pottery. Apache culture will probably reveal similar borrowings, though more random ones. How far there was reaction upon the Pueblos is as yet less clear. Their culture has been avowedly on the defensive for three or four centuries, and probably so in the grain for as long before. Yet some discernible interaction is expectable.

The relation of the two sets of peoples has numerous parallels: in modern east Africa, in India, between ancient Canaanite and Israelite, between still older Mesopotamian valley and hill or desert dweller. It seems to begin to reappear in parts of Central and South America. It does seem unique for North America. The antecedent condition appears to be a culture of long and settled tradition, town or at least soil bound, self-centered and nonexpansive, differentiating from a more generalized culture.

When it comes to external relations of the Southwest, the outstanding problem of course is the connection with southern Mexico. Everyone has always been aware of this; and yet almost no progress has been made in understanding the relation. There are two reasons.

The first reason is anthropological ignorance of northern Mexico. The result is that almost all our distributions are interrupted by blanks, which an occasional report for the Tarahumare or Huichol, or of a border ruin like La Quemada and Chalchihuites, does not seriously dissipate. It is the remote northern half of the Southwest which we are compelled to compare with the Mexican center of higher culture.

Perhaps still more important is the chaos of understanding of southern Mexico. There has been valuable work by specialists, under the leadership of Seler. There has been no real attempt to order the older ethnological data and to comprehend them in all their relations—data which are easily the fullest and most valuable left by the conquerors and colonizers of any area in the hemisphere. The archaeology is in equally bad shape. The one brilliant exception is the progress made in the unraveling of Maya history. And yet, granting the exactness of the chronology—and this is not yet beyond dispute—there is a danger, perhaps an illusion, in the beam of illumination that streams down the vista of Maya history. It shows us dates, linked with and corroborated by developments in art, architecture, and calendar. The dates are probably linkable with stages in other phases of Maya culture—pottery and textiles, agriculture and trade, perhaps ritual and institutions. But the linkage has not yet been made. And as soon as we pass beyond the Maya, defined relations are random; largely limited to the vague concept of Toltec, in fact. Not that the results of work in Maya chronology are unimportant. They constitute easily the most significant line of historical evidence available for the history of pre-Columbian America. But their full significance lies in the light they will shed on Mexico as a whole, and through this serve as a scale by which the remainder of the culture of the hemisphere will be measurable. And Mexico cannot be really illumined by Maya chronology until its own house is put in order. Reciprocally, the Maya growth, so obviously an integral part of the larger Mexican one, will get its complete meaning, to which dates can contribute only one element, out of this relation. The danger lies in overestimating the proportion of the whole task already accomplished. The remedy is systematic attack of the Mexican situation as a whole in one aspect after another.

How little knowledge we really control is clear as soon as we turn attention to any one people or any one activity of culture. Seler and Krickeberg have shown what information can be assembled on even the so-called lesser populations such as the Tarasca and Totonac. But there is nothing comparable available on the Otomi, on the important Nahua-speaking groups outside the Valley of Mexico, nor even on the Zapotecan area, generally recognized as the most advanced after Maya and Mexican proper. On the side of separate lines of culture, the obscurity prevailing as to metallurgy and ceramic types is sufficient reminder of the situation. In pottery we are still dealing with the vague and locally variable concepts of Archaic, Toltec-Teotihuacan, and Aztec horizons, while Pueblo prehistory is organized into seven well defined successions. Finds of Mexican pottery and metal in Pueblo ruins of known period lose most of their significance for comparison because there is as yet no real Mexican prehistory.

In fact, there is a possibility of Southwestern coming to the rescue of Mexican chronology through such cross-tying specimens. Douglass, in his work on tree growth,[31] has carried a year identification system for the American Southwest back to 1300. Beyond this by an unknown interval, he has a floating block of several centuries of identifiable year growths. In this block belong rafters from Pueblo ruins, such as Aztec and Bonito, of the third or Great Pueblo period. As it is the fourth period into which the Spanish Conquest falls, and the beginning of this period can scarcely be assumed to lie more than a few centuries earlier, it seems probable that the end of the floating block in which the third-period ruins fall, cannot be much anterior to 1300. A reasonable supply of timbers from late third or early fourth period ruins would therefore in all probability close the gap and give a year by year record back to at least A.D. 1000 into which rafter-bearing ruins could be tied. This record in turn, through occasional Mexican trade pieces associated with such ruins, would reflect on Mexican conditions of general Toltec era, and perhaps enable confirmation of one or more of the conflicting legendary chronologies that have come down to us through the Aztecs. It will be necessary, however, for the tree-growth dating record to be published in full, and for its technique to be controllable by several investigators, before its results are likely to be accepted without reservation.

As regards progress in its relating to the higher Mexican center, then, the Southwest is primarily dependent on further study of Mexico. As regards relations of the Southwest to the remainder of the continent, the situation is different.

On account of the geographical position of the Southwest, its relative degree of general cultural advancement, and certain specific similarities with Mexico, such as masonry, painted pottery, cloth-weaving, rain ceremonies, priesthood, and the like, it has been customary to regard the Southwest as the gateway through which passed or filtered most of the cultural flow from the higher centers of Middle America to the remoter portions of the continent. As to the reality of this flow as regards most pre-Columbian advancement, Boas, Wissler, in fact practically all American students, seem in agreement. Independent local evolutions along this or that line have of course been recognized; also reciprocal influences between northwestern America and northeastern Asia; and some flow via the Antilles into the Southeast of the United States.[32] But in the main the concept seems to have been, at least implicitly, of a radiating transmission to and through the Southwest.

Hand in hand with this concept, though not logically associated with it, has gone another: the picture of North American culture as divisible into some ten types or blocks, each contained in the regional frame of a culture area. The recognition of these areal types of culture began empirically, grew gradually without program or much methodological review, but was so general that when Wissler's definitive formulation was made,[33] it evoked neither dissent nor the enthusiasm of discovery. However, it is increasingly clear that the familiar culture areas are useful tools only up to a certain point. They are not equivalent in historic depth. The Plateau type of culture is obviously not to be put on a level with the Southwestern as regards either richness or productive originality. It represents a different level of development. It has been and is primarily passive or receptive in its relations with the cultures of other areas. The northern or Columbia-Frazer portion of the Plateau is a hinterland to the Northwest Coast, and at the same time to the northern Plains.[34] The southern or Great Basin portion is similarly a hinterland or part of the central Californian culture, with Southwestern and central Plains traits in reduction also entering it from the south and east.[35] The two halves of the Plateau really have little in common other than a low level of undifferentiated culture. They resemble each other in lacks much more than in common specific traits. It is plain that the Plateau "culture area" therefore represents a formulation of a different order from the Northwest or Southwest.

Recognizing facts of this nature, Boas, Spinden, and some others see little significance in the culture area other than as a mechanism of transient convenience for descriptive classification. On the other hand, Wissler has made a pretty strong showing for the approximate coincidence of areas plotted independently from the archaeological and ethnological approach; in other words, the areal types are likely to be long lived. He has also defined environment as a factor stabilizing a culture in an area and tending to restrict it to that area.[36]

The issues thus raised involve deeper problems of historic method than justice can be done to in passing. It may be admitted however that there has been a lack of integration in Americanistic studies between the dealing with culture areas on the one hand, in which broader historic questions have been dimmed by the intensive local approach or by descriptive considerations; and on the other, inquiries into problems of continental history, which have either remained summary or have been limited to distributional investigations of one set of elements at a time. The culture aggregations defined by areas will by themselves of course never reconstruct the general American sequence of events. Yet they have proved themselves too well substantiated to make their ignoring wise or profitable in the larger task.

One way of breaking the deadlock is to accept the areas but refuse to treat them any longer as historic equivalents. The way has been pointed by Wissler in his recognition of culture centers rather than culture areas.[37] This approach can perhaps be carried out more consistently. Further, the concept of center can be applied to the relations between areas, instead of remaining restricted to the nuclei or focal points within areas. A whole area is conceivable as a center toward one or more other areas. There is nothing radically new in this concept. It has been quite generally held as regards the relation of Middle America to the remainder of the hemisphere. It is capable of application to areas like the Southwest in their historic relations to areas like the Plateau; just as it is applicable again to the relations of strains or subareas of culture within the Southwest—the Pueblo, the Gila-Sonoran, the southern California littoral, for instance. In this way the overly descriptive or static view of culture areas can be given a "dynamic" or processual or sequential significance and yet have its findings remain intensive and exact to a greater degree than the necessarily somewhat averaged and sketchy conclusions resulting from the broad continental approach.

Attempting then to see things from this viewpoint, we find north of southern Mexico three principal centers of cultural productivity and differentiation, each corresponding approximately to an accepted culture area. These three centers are the Northwest, Southwest, and Southeast. On these three the half-dozen other areas have been essentially dependent in much the same way that most of the continent has been dependent in a larger way on southern Mexico.

Of the three, the Northwest Coast stands most apart historically.[38] Its lack of the agriculture and pottery of Mexico and the two other centers, long recognized, is significant. But at point after point a similar distinctiveness is manifest: the use of adzes instead of axes for instance, the game forms and month counts, the technology and patterning of art, the basketry twining with superstructural ornamentation, the special local inceptions of weaving and the use of metal, the whole fabric of social valuing of the economics of life. Whatever is not simple and more or less universal or primitive in Northwest culture, is, generally speaking, of either local or Asiatic origin. Between these two possibilities, a decision cannot always be rendered at present. It seems likely that more and more of the material of Northwest culture will prove to rest upon Asiatic export, although mostly so thoroughly reworked on the spot in accord with local patterns, as to be identifiable only after considerable analysis. Less and less of its specific content, on the other hand, seems to point to origins from or even relation with the south.

The Southwest and Southeast belong admittedly to the great block of truly American culture culminating in the Middle or sub-Isthmian region. They represent as it were limbs from the same trunk. It is their relations to this trunk and to each other that need elucidation.

The Southwest shares with southern Mexico the planter, metate, and tortilla elements of maize growing and use; the domesticated turkey; painted pottery; masonry; cotton, cloth-weaving, and textile clothing; and strong tendencies toward ritualization, including altars, priesthood, masks. It lacks totally metals, town courts and pyramidal substructures, ability to construct political fabrics, and oratory, all of which are not only Mexican but Southeastern.

Certain Southeastern traits seem either derived or due to stimulation from the Antilles and ultimately from South America: the quasi metallurgy, the hoe and wooden mortar in relation to maize, modeling and incising of pottery, the blowgun.[39] So far as can be seen today, however, only part of Southeastern culture can be led back to a South American origin. The pyramid, confederacy, oratory, religiously founded caste distinctions and sun cult among the Natchez, scaffold sacrifice, perhaps the style of carved gorgets, point to Mexico. It seems dubious that these traits came in via the Southwest and then were lost there; or that they entered analogously through the West Indies. The alternatives, unless coincidence be accepted, are sea communication from southern Mexico to the northern coast of the Gulf of Mexico, or transmission through Tamaulipas and Texas, a badly explored stretch to date not reported as containing evidences of remains that would serve as links.[40]

Primarily the unraveling of this problem concerns specialists in the Southeast. But it is bound to be of bearing also on the history of the Southwest. We scarcely know by direct evidence even the eastern limit of former Pueblo culture. General Southwestern radiations ought to be traceable farther than they are traceable. The pottery which the Texas coast seems to afford has not been placed in its relationships. In the Ozark region of Arkansas Harrington has recently found a "Bluff-dweller" culture showing Southeastern and still more numerous Southwestern traits.[41] There may be more such linkage material, and if so it is historically important. Thus it is chiefly in and about the Arkansas area[42] that pottery of Southeastern type manifested an inclination toward painted decoration.

However, the cultural centers of the two areas lie respectively on or beyond the upper Rio Grande and the lower Mississippi; and in the long intervening stretch culture appears always to have been less differentiated and more simple. There is therefore little doubt that we are dealing with two essentially distinct hearths. Their behavior outward is also different. The Southwestern culture has been nonexpansive; its Pueblo form conspicuously so. Agriculture is ancient in the area—older than pueblos; yet has never become established even in southern California. Central California has received elements, but has not been impressed by the stamp of the Southwest. The Great Basin tribes appear to be about as simple culturally as they were several thousand years ago; and yet Paiute are virtual neighbors of the Hopi. In the Plains there are some traits that can presumably be led back to a Southwestern origin: earth altars, for instance, dice-scoring on a circuit, perhaps the fetish bundle and shields. In the main, however, it is remarkable how little the Plains seem to have taken over from the Southwest. The reciprocal influence seems at least equal; since the introduction of the horse, probably more powerful. Taos, the frontier settlement, is counted Pueblo and essentially is such; but in material culture and dress it is half Plains. Taos has evidently absorbed Plains culture to much the degree that Ácoma and Zuñi have absorbed Spanish Mexican culture. As normally it is the more advanced culture that affects the other most, Southwestern impulses are indicated as unusually self-contained, centripedal, perhaps weak in all respects except tenacity.

The Southeast, on the other hand, can be regarded as having the Northeast and Plains tributary to it; at any rate, as being that part of a large eastern area in which culture culminated. The distinction between the Northeast and Southeast is constantly making trouble. The Northern Woodland is little else than a simplified copy of the Southern, practicing southern agriculture as far north as the geography permitted, and beyond that showing a few positive traits unrepresented in Gulf drainage. The systematized archaeological results in New York yield three horizons.[43] The first, called Algonkin, is similar to that of the historic peripheral tribes. The second, or Mound Builder, is the northeastern outpost of a culture centering, in its specific form, in the Ohio Valley, and connected thence with the middle and lower Mississippi and also with the headwaters of the Gulf drainage to the south, as for instance Moorehead's distribution maps of stone ornaments make conveniently clear.[44] The third or Iroquoian horizon is that of a people proved to have southern speech relatives in the Cherokee, and possessing a culture that at point after point is still southeastern: confederate organization, pottery types, blowgun, and so forth. Evidently then there have been a series of waves northward out of the Gulf region, some migrational, some perhaps essentially and actively cultural, which, with a diffusing seepage in the same direction, have given the Northeast what it has other than of the simplest. The historical situation is best represented by the employment for both Southeast and Northeast of the single term Woodland—as indeed its frequent usage suggests. Recognition of southern, northern, and perhaps other subareas or phases amplifies without disturbing recognition of the substantial unity of this eastern or Woodland culture.

In the Plains a relatively recent shift seems to have partly disguised the underlying relationship. The largely negative results of archaeology indicate the Plains as only sparsely or intermittently inhabited for a long time. The population was probably in the main a Woodland one along the eastern margin. These peoples presumably at various times pushed westward along the timbered stream bottoms, learning more and more to hunt and travel after the bison, but chiefly seasonally, their residence and farming remaining in the bottoms. Offshoots occasionally wandered farther, and now and then remained as isolated "village tribes" like the Mandan and Hidatsa. Enough remembrance of such permanent adventures may have been kept alive to cause the Arikara to follow them, if indeed they did not set the example. The western Plains on the whole were still little utilized in this early period. Some Basin and Plateau groups had probably spilled over, but kept essentially to the base of the Rocky Mountains. The highest development was almost certainly in the south, among Caddoans and southern Siouans or tribes that may have preceded them, in contact with the lower Mississippi groups.

Then, about 1650, came the horse, which could be taken over with immense profit and without serious readjustment by the bison-hunting, dog-traveling tribes. Population, wealth, and leisure increased rapidly, and there was a florescence of culture. The material side of life acquired a certain sumptuousness; the warfare of eastern type was made over into a specialized system with refined social values; rituals and societies multiplied and acquired some magnificence; or developed elaborations like age-grading. The western Plains became as utilizable as the eastern, and before long the whole tract to the Rockies was occupied and a strong influence exerted on the nearer Basin and Plateau peoples. This change was still going on in the period of exploration and first white settlement. By the time ethnologists arrived it had begun to be succeeded by the phase of disintegration due to Caucasian contact, and the process, or even its recency, was no longer patent, so that the earlier scientific accounts are statically descriptive, in the main.

In this Indian summer culmination of Plains culture it was the remoter tribes that forged ahead fastest: The Algonkins and north Siouans. Possibly the southern groups participated less actively because they already possessed older, fuller, and richer culture patterns: they took on less because they had more to lose by the change. Perhaps too their culture had already begun to be undermined by indirect French and Spanish contacts. At any rate, the American settlement hit them first, they began to crumble, and field anthropologists turned their main attention to the less spoiled northern tribes. It is these factors that have made the focus of Plains culture appear to lie in the north and west about the upper Missouri and along the base of the Rockies, among Teton Dakota and Crow, Cheyenne and Arapaho, Blackfoot and Gros Ventre, Mandan and Hidatsa, as Wissler's reviews show.[45] Two to four centuries earlier, it probably lay south of the Platte. It might even prove to have lain there as late as the nineteenth century if the data had been collected so as to enable our approaching the Plains complex from the point of view of its southern rather than its northern ingredients.

Granted the substantial correctness of this view, we see the most specific traits of Plains culture resolving into the products of a transitory development which lies wholly between the first stimulating indirect

Caucasian influences and their final direct and destroying ones: the result of a cultural intoxication. The Plains traits that have historic depth, on the other hand, seem Woodland, and date from the time when such Plains culture as there was constituted a margin at the fringe of a natural area. The forces which infused this marginal culture, like those of the northern and eastern margins, had their heads in the Southeast.

On this basis traits of Plains culture can be explained whose occurrence otherwise is random and meaningless. The matrilineate of the Pawnee and of the Hidatsa-Crow group, for instance, would be historically connected with that of the Natchez, Muskogi, and Cherokee in a distribution once continuous—like that of the Iroquois—instead of our having to explain the anomaly of four separate matrilinear areas east of the hundredth meridian.

With the facts arranged in this perspective, the relation of the Southeastern and Southwestern culture hearths presents a new set of problems.

The eastern Gulf Coast region becomes the most intensive focus of a culture growth covering the continent east of the Rocky Mountains up to the limits at which stringent environment has kept life simple, composed mainly of ancient elements, and relatively unsusceptible to foreign influences except such as have passed through the filter of cultures adjusted to a similar environment in Asia. The original sources of the growth at its center are composite: probably Antillean-South American, Mexican, and Mexican via the Southwest.

The Southwest, to the contrary, nearer the Mexican center, seems to have received material mainly or only from this center, to have evolved or modified from it essentially through internal causes, and to have had an unusually feeble sphere or direct influences, limited to partial transmissions, never dominant ones, into immediately adjacent areas. Situated at the gateway out of Mexico, it has passed little culture through; or, if in greater amount, in such form that the origin of the material is disguised and difficult to recognize. Into the formation of the Southwestern culture has gone an ancient one, that of the Basketmakers, which is more or less represented also in the Basin and in California, is analogous at least in level and economic type to that of the Plateau, and may have extended much farther. Out of the blending of Basketmaker and Mexican material, the Southwest constructed its own special culture, without imparting the product to the outside on any notable scale. Southwest culture as such did not even come to extend over more than part of the area once occupied by the Basketmaker or Plateau-type culture. Why this areal restriction occurred, why the eastern growth behaved differently from the Southwestern, how far the two may after all have been interconnected under the surface, are problems before us.

Impingements from outside the continent on the Southwest seem few. So far as can be told in the present state of knowledge, little or nothing of ultimate South American origin reached our area. It shares with Mexico many of the Middle American traits which seem to be of south Mexican origin: maize and the rectangular metate, the turkey, rain rituals, are examples. To the contrary, metallurgy, which is beginning to be recognized as outstandingly a South American development, and which may have reached Mexico late,[46] is not represented in the Southwest at all. Similarly with the slit drum, the Pan's pipe, the blowgun, the stool and the litter, perhaps certain weaving processes, whose distribution suggests their South American origin and some of which got a foothold in Mexico.

Asiatic culture traits also are practically absent in the Southwest. The sinew-backed bow, frequently accepted as a form of the Asiatic composite bow, has its farthest and somewhat hesitating occurrence in the Southwest. The magic flight and earth-diving tales, the conical or tripod-foundation dwelling, dog-traction, fitted clothing and in the main the moccasin, all of which have an Asiatic as well as American distribution, are not characteristic of the Southwest.

Transpacific influences are hardly expectable for recognition in the Southwest as a whole; but there are one or two interesting possibilities in southern California. Outstanding is the cosmogony of the Luiseño and perhaps Gabrielino. It begins with semipersonifications of abstract states or qualities which continue in a succession of aeons or generationlike existences and finally incarnate in Heaven and Earth, from whom all beings are born in a long series of parturitions.[47] The pattern is thoroughly Polynesian in character, and without parallel in America. Either an Oceanic influence or an extraordinary coincidence has therefore occurred. The Gabrielino and Chumash also had shell fishhooks of strictly Micronesian form. Here, however, specific resemblances seem to end; so that we have at most the remnant of a sporadic influence, not any determinant or essential molding of the culture from across the ocean.

The effect of the Caucasian has of course been a different story; but even toward him the Southwest has manifested its usual self-centering and defensive tenacity. No region north of Mexico was so early invaded and settled and has kept so much of its native culture intact as the Southwest. Pueblo and Navaho, Apache and Papago, Tarahumare and Yaqui have absorbed a great number of Latin traits, yet have maintained the fabric of their old life to a surprising extent. Occidental culture forms a large part of the content; native culture is still the container.

A careful analysis of this absorption or hybridization should yield unusually interesting results, both as an unfolding narrative and with reference to the processes involved. Ethnologists have called attention to many of the elements of Latin origin, even the less obvious ones; but they have done so primarily in order to clear the sought for picture of the old native culture from its late intrusions. Historians have also dealt with the contacts; but in the main the Indian, whether friend, foe, neighbor, subject, or convert, is to the documentary historian material on which Caucasian institutions have played in their local developments. In the one case the Spanish ingredient was something to be recognized in order to be discounted; in the other, the Indian was the occasion of the plot rather than its theme. A systematic sociological examination of the contact as such still remains to be made.

Such seem to be the more outstanding and immediate problems of the Southwest as the cumulative results of anthropological work in the last generation have brought them to the fore.

PART 10

# INTRODUCTION

In this intriguing paper which was published in 1933, Elsie Clews Parsons holds forth the rather captivating, inferential theory that Aztec and Pueblo Indian religious practices contained sufficient parallelism as to suggest syncretic action from Mesoamerica to the Southwest. While stopping short of a flat statement that such syncretism did occur, she builds a case—through example—that is most difficult to ignore, let alone dismiss out of hand.

Most earlier theory as to any syncretism in religious practice had imputed such a blend—at least among the Pueblos—to early Spanish influence in the Southwest.[1] In this presentation, however, example after example of parallel rites, dances, or ceremonies are specifically cited, which lead the reader to the conclusion that either there was an inordinate amount of multigenesis of religious practices or that there was, indeed, a great amount of culture transfer from Mesoamerica—specifically from the Aztecs—to groups in the Southwest; the Pueblos in this instance.

The comparisons—with contrasts duly noted—between the Aztec and Pueblo groups range from systems of communal service to pantheons of like gods to identical or highly similar instances of religious practice. Basing herself primarily on the early Spanish ethnographer, Sahagún, Parsons deductively reasons that Tlaloc cults of central Mexico and the Kachina cults of the Pueblo groups have much more intertwined similarity than anyone had previously suspected. Citing masks, dances, ceremonies, and godly attributes, Parsons builds such a striking case that one must be at least impressed with the possibility of Mesoamerican-Southwest influence.

The author compares, for example, the Aztec "old men" and the Hopi chiefs, both of whom performed a new fire ceremony; she indicates that the performance of ceremonies in long or short forms is an Aztec-Hopi parallel, and she points out that, while the Pueblos were indifferent to a year-count such as that used by the Aztecs, both groups had a similar interval in timing ceremonies, with the possibility that "every eight years" or "every four years" used by the Aztecs may have been the same as the similarly loose "every four years" of the Hopi-Zuñi calendars.

Parsons does make clear that in spite of the vast number of parallels in ceremonial matters, it has not been possible to equate large ceremonial complexes which, in fact, differ widely among Pueblos themselves, as well as among various central Mexican groups. There is one exception to this general statement, and that is the comparison of the Shalako and the twelfth month Aztec ceremony called Teotleco. Here the points of similarity are, in Parson's mind, extraordinarily close and impressive.

Although Parsons draws no particular conclusions from her material, except to retreat from her previous position that Southwestern ceremonialism had been largely affected by Mesoamerica after Spanish contact, research of the last forty years gives us new perspective on this matter. In the first place, as Parsons undoubtedly realized, her comparisons were probably not between "Aztecs" and Pueblo, but represent contacts over a much longer period, which can only be observed in full detail on an ethnohistoric level. There does seem to be a possibility, however, that the Zuñi ceremony of the Kokowaia or Shalako may be a late introduction from Mexico and so, indeed, may be more or less influenced by Aztec or some neighboring people. However, it is also conceivable that the Shalako ceremony was, in part or in whole, introduced in post-Spanish times since the Zuñi pueblos seem to have received most of the Indians who remained behind from the Coronado party. From our scanty evidence, we do know that some of these were either Aztec or from nearby, Nahautl-speaking groups.[2]

Balancing this latter suggestion to some extent, however, is our growing realization of the great time depth of specific Mesoamerican ceremonials in western Zacatecas, virtually on the southern border of the Greater Southwest and the northwestern periphery of Mesoamerica.[3]

Some items mentioned by Parsons are of special interest as the result of the increase in our knowledge of the archaeology of both the Southwest and northwestern Mesoamerica since she wrote this article. Thus, she notes that an older Mesoamerican cult concept emphasizing the association of gods with the cardinal directions is represented by Pueblo chiefs of the directions intimately associated with mountain tops as were the corresponding Tlalocs (or other deities) in Mesoamerica. But, she states, this cult in the Southwest is largely associated with, but somewhat obscured by, the Kachina cult, which had not spread over the entire Pueblo region. From this she infers that the cult of the directional gods may have been introduced earlier into the Southwest followed by a latter introduction of the Kachina cult which partially merged with the earlier cult. Such a conclusion is strikingly confirmed by more recent archaeological findings. Thus from our own work in Mexico we know that during the period circa A.D. 300–750 the peripherally Mesoamerican Chalchihuites culture in Zacatecas and Durango emphasized in ceramic design and inferentially in ceremonialism the concept of the four world quarters, with gods depicted in two or four opposed quadrants in bowl interior decoration. The oldest interior decorated bowls in Hohokam and to a certain extent in

Mogollon-Anasazi cultures used the same quadrate interior design, although usually without god depictions. Stylistic traits indicate the origin of some Southwestern traits in these cultures of northwestern Mexico, and recent analysis of the turquoise used in the Mexican cultures for jewelry demonstrates that the turquoise itself had originated in the aboriginal Cerrillos turquoise mines south of Santa Fe, New Mexico,[4] clearly linking the Anasazi and Chalchihuites cultures in a trade relationship prior to A.D. 750. Almost certainly, the concept—and cult—of the gods of the cardinal directions was introduced in the Southwest by that time, if not earlier.

Also, for some years, evidence has been accumulating pointing to the movement of a wave of nuclear Mesoamerican ceremonialism, most likely as one aspect of the organization of a new Mesoamerica-Southwestern *pochteca*-like trade route, up the west coast of Mexico, essentially between A.D. 1000 and 1400.[5] This influence spread to Guasave in northern Sinaloa and thence across the Sierra Madre Occidental to Puebloan settlements at Casas Grandes, which quickly became a *pochteca* center for trade into the Southwest.[6] In 1943, Brew (article reproduced elsewhere in this volume) noted that just such a wave of ceremonialism evidenced primarily by ceramic decoration and kiva mural painting, had arrived in the Southwest at the very end of Pueblo III and the beginning of Pueblo IV. Brew specifically equated this ceremonialism with the Tlaloc cult of Mesoamerica and the Kachina cult of the Southwest and to some extent attributed what actually amounted to a renaissance of Puebloan culture during Pueblo IV to this source. A number of archaeological finds in various parts of the Southwest have now clearly established the existence of the Kachina cult there during at least late Pueblo III and Pueblo IV. Parsons's hesitant but brilliant suggestion now appears fully substantiated.

Similarly, her perceptive recognition that the canes of authority of the Pueblos did not originate with the Spanish *varas* but were aboriginal cult items of considerable antiquity in the Southwest and were probably to be equated with the canes of the Aztec Pochteca has been strongly reinforced by archaeological finds. Hampered, in her day, by a lack of the archaeological evidence for Mesoamerican influence on the Southwest and similar evidence for the great time depth of Puebloan ceremonialism, Parsons nevertheless was able in this paper to arrive at some amazingly correct suggestions and conclusions regarding relationships between the two cultural spheres.

# 14

# SOME AZTEC AND PUEBLO PARALLELS

### Elsie Clews Parsons

In rereading Sahagún's *History of Ancient Mexico* in the translation recently published by Mrs. Bandelier[1] I have been struck by the number of parallels between Aztec and Pueblo cultures, some of which, as far as I know, have never been pointed out.

In both cultures impersonation of the gods is an outstanding trait, impersonation by priests or by persons who play the part for one year whether as among the Aztec they are prisoners destined for final sacrifice, or as among the Pueblo they are war captains representing the war gods, or sacred clowns who are very well paid at the close of their culminating ceremony, or men designated to wear the masks of Kachina rain spirits like the Zuñi Shalako. With few exceptions impersonation among the Aztec appears to have been without mask; among the Pueblo the use of masks is so prominent a trait among both annual and occasional impersonations that the role of impersonation without mask such as played by Bitsitsi of the Zuñi Ne'wekwe and by Muyingwa, the male corn spirit of the Hopi, by the Hopi Powamu Kachina, or by the turtle dancers of San Juan or Taos, tends to be overlooked.

Whatever the origin of the Pueblo mask, there is no doubt that its efflorescence has been comparatively recent and that this was stimulated by the Spanish use of masks. Among the Hopi, certain masks are never worn and these I would compare with the pre-Conquest Mexican masks in stone or metal which were too heavy or too small to have been worn in ceremonial. The use of masks by dance impersonators I have imputed elsewhere[2] to Spanish influence. But now in Sahagún I find an account of a mask worn in impersonation and in the very cult where the mask flourishes most among the Pueblos—the rain god or Kachina cult. At the head of the procession to the temple walked the priest of the god Tlaloc.

> He wore on the head a crown shaped like a casquet, adjusted about the temples and widening towards the top; from the center of this crown

> rose many plumes. His face was smeared with liquid ulli (gum) which in this state is black like ink; . . . he also wore a very ugly mask with a big nose, and a mane of hair down to the waist; this hair wig was inserted in the mask.[3]

The long hair and the black face paint are Pueblo mask traits. To my mind here is stronger evidence for belief that the Kachina dance mask was pre-Spanish[4] than the statement of Luxán that the Tiguas used many masks in their dances and ceremonies.[5] This statement was made in 1582 and there is a possibility that the Spanish mask had spread. Besides, Luxán does not state how the mask was actually used, and it is unlikely that he himself saw any mask, at least in use, since the Indians fled at the approach of the Spaniards.

Tlaloc, or rather the Tlaloco, the Aztec rain gods, were associated with the cardinal directions, as are the Hopi cloud youths or the Zuñi Uwannami, rain chiefs of the directions. The Pueblo chiefs of the directions are intimately associated with mountaintops as were the Tlalocs. There *are* distinctions between the chiefs of the directions and the Kachina in Pueblo religion, but they are often obscure; perhaps two cults have merged, and the older cult, that of the chiefs of the directions, has been blurred by the later one, that of the Kachina which has not yet spread over the entire Pueblo region.

The rain chiefs of the directions (Uwannami of Zuñi, cloud youths of the Hopi, Shiwanna of the Keres, Liwane of the Tanoans) are to be more closely equated with the Tlalocs than are the Kachina. However, in the Tlaloc cult there is one trait which is peculiarly close to a trait in the Kachina cult—curing for certain diseases. Curing by the Kachina has been somewhat overlooked until recently,[6] and just why they are called upon to cure is not known. I think the following passage from Sahagún is highly suggestive.

> All prominent mountain peaks, especially such around which rain clouds will gather, they imagine to be gods. They also thought that certain diseases which are due to the cold or inclement weather came from the mountains, and that these mountains had the power to cure them. Therefore, all those who became ill of such diseases [rheumatism, paralysis, blotches] made a vow to offer a feast and offering to such and such a mountain closest to which they happened to live, or to which they were most devoted.[7]

The Hopi practice of having a dance (a Kachina dance or water serpent dance-ceremony) when there is sickness in the family[8] is a pretty close parallel to this Aztec "vow." It is a common Aztec-Pueblo attitude that those who cause a disease also cure it.[9]

Aztec curers or curing groups—Sahagún is obscure on their organization[10]—were distinct from the priests or priesthoods, as Pueblo, notably Zuñi, shamans or curing societies are distinct from the priesthoods or rain chieftaincies; but this matter of organization among the Pueblo has been very much complicated by inter-Pueblo borrowing and is too intricate to go into here. Suffice it to say that there is a trend toward separation of functions among both peoples. I surmise that ideologically in both cultures if a supernatural cause the disease, his priest is to be called upon to cure it; if a witch cause it, another witch or doctor will be called upon to cure. Aztec curers extracted worms and small pebbles,[11] just as do Pueblo curers, and probably in the ways the Pueblos do, by brushing with feathers and by sucking. Although Sahagún does not specify what he means by extracting, it seems fairly certain that it was by one or both of these ways—Zapotecas and Mixtecas today cure by sucking out deleterious objects,[12] as do the Cora and Huichol, and all these peoples were in contact with the Aztec. Cora and Huichol also brush with feathers.[13]

The Aztec had various ideas about the afterlife, as have the Pueblo; but Tlalocan, the home of the rain gods, may be equated with the "earthly paradise" of the Pueblo, with Wenima, in describing which Father Dumarest uses almost the same terms as Father Bernardino.[14] To Tlalocan go persons killed by lightning, those who are drowned, the lepers, those afflicted with pustules, the mangy, the gout-stricken, and those with dropsy.[15] Now among the Pueblo there are hints that not all the dead become Kachina. A heavy rainstorm after a man's death indicates that he has become a Kachina;[16] the rain priests of Zuñi have more to do with rainfall after death than the ordinary dead; within priesthoods and curing societies special prayer sticks are made for the deceased members, suggesting that they have become spirits distinct from the dead at large; the prayer stick for the dead is distinct from the prayer stick for the Kachina. In Pueblo burial, distinctions are made between ceremonialists and non-ceremonialists. At Isleta the deceased ceremonialist has ritual performed for him by his ceremonial group. In general the faces of deceased ceremonialists are painted as in life and some of their paraphernalia may be buried with them. At Zuñi a man's personal mask is buried (apart from his body) and the corn fetish or "mother" of the curing society member is buried. Presumably these things are to be used after death, their owners continuing to function after death as in life.[17] Now let us return to the Aztec who went to Tlalocan. They were buried, not burned. Wild amaranth seeds were put on their jaw (this no doubt was food for their journey); blue[18] paint was put on their forehead with cut-up papers; other papers were put behind the head; a cane was placed in one hand (this, too, probably for the journey). Sahagún gives no explanation for the special treatment of these persons, but as their spirits are bound for Tlalocan it is extremely probable that they are to become rain spirits. The Tlalocs are impersonated by their long-haired priests. My guess is that both priests and the afflicted who have been treated by these priests become Tlalocs. If so, we have here several elements of the Pueblo curing society, particularly the society engaged in curing for lightning shock or for skin disease.

The concept of the drowned becoming rain or water spirits calls for special discussion. Among modern Nahuatl-speaking communities wells (springs) or tanks are believed to be haunted or lived in by water spirits. In Ixtapalapan, probably the most Aztec of all the suburbs of Mexico City, I heard of a fish youth coming out of a well to court a girl, to whose parents he gave a little carp of gold. After being married at the well by the *cura*, the couple sank down into the water.

We recall the Zuñi-Hopi tales of the horned water serpent who seduces maidens[19] and to whom when he sent flood a girl and a boy were sacrificed.[20] This flood-sending serpent has been found among the Mayo-Yaqui[21] and among the Zapoteca,[22] where he is also a horned serpent and lives in springs or wells and rivers and receives offerings. The chief suggestion of human sacrifice among the Pueblo is in association with the horned water serpent or with pools,[23] and we can but think that it is an echo from the south.[24] Possibly the incident in the Keresan tale of the competing Earth Mothers, where Younger Sister takes out the heart of Older Sister[25] is another echo, an even remoter echo. There are other Pueblo tales of taking out the heart, substituting a good heart for a bad one, and the Hopi have a tradition about burying the heart of a human enemy.

Here I am tempted into an hypothesis on the still unexplained facts of human sacrifice among the Aztec, an hypothesis suggested by Pueblo scalp ideology and ritual. Pueblo scalp ceremonial was an initiation of the dead enemy into the tribe in order that he might become a rainmaker, a potent rain spirit to aid his adoptive people. (At Isleta the scalps also cure toothache and give warning of the approach of enemies.)[26] I suggest that the Aztec treatment of captives was homologous, at least in the case of those who were considered impersonations of the god. They were treated as impersonations before death because after death they were to join the gods, become gods.[27] This may have been the starting point, the cell which later took on the cancerous growth which so differentiated the

Aztec from other Indian cultures. Child sacrifice to the mountain rain gods would seem to have been part of such later development.[28]

Apart from human sacrifice, Pueblo or northern war ritual is found among the Aztec. We may compare the impaling of heads on poles[29] with the scalp pole, noting that in Hopi tradition taking a head[30] is mentioned more often than taking a scalp, and that the Natashka masks pretend to cut off the head of a captive.[31] Cutting off the head (as well as cutting out the heart and other organs) occurs also in Zuñi and Keresan myths.[32] The Aztec danced with the head; the Pueblo danced around the scalp pole. The Laguna scalp-taker had to wear a piece of the skin of the victim until the close of the scalp dance,[33] which suggests an Aztec practice. Heads (before decapitation) or scalps are fed.[34] Heads or scalps are kept in a temple or house (shrine).[35] (The scalps taken in Zippe's ceremony were kept in private houses "as a relic.")[36] In both cultures arrows are offered to the war gods,[37] miniature arrows at Zuñi, and we may note that in Mexico the diminutive offering is a very marked trait.[38] Mutual taunting by the old women and the young men and warriors is another Aztec-Pueblo war trait.[39]

The ritual of blood sacrifice[40] is so conspicuous and so dominant among the Aztecs that it tends to obscure comparison between the Aztec and other Indian cultures lacking[41] the blood complex; nevertheless between the Aztec and the Pueblo there are many ritual similarities. Fasting and continence are both Aztec and Pueblo traits and such abstinence is observed for four ritual days, a "retreat" which concludes with the dance on the fifth day.[42] Fasting may consist of one meal a day, or certain ordinary food elements may be omitted like lime in cooking corn (Aztec), or chili (Aztec), or salt (Zuñi, Hopi). Variations are played upon ritual abstinence among both Aztec and Pueblo.[43] The periods of taboo may vary; they may precede or follow the ceremonial. Comestibles may be served or dressed in special ways or eaten formally, e.g., by four mouthfuls. When the continence taboo is broken, venereal disease results or the mask will stick to the face.[44] In both cultures, exorcism[45] is expressed by spitting and throwing from the hands,[46] by the use of ashes, and by bathing, to wash off ritual paint,[47] etc.; offerings are made of bread "fashioned into diverse figures"; food offering is thrown into the fire;[48] food is offered to fetishes;[49] blood is smeared on their mouths;[50] cornmeal is strewn;[51] popcorn is used ritualistically;[52] as noted, miniature offerings are in vogue;[53] there is an offering of incense or tobacco-filled canes or cigarettes;[54] images, impersonators (or their masks) are smoked;[55] smoke is swallowed,[56] a practice referred to in Pueblo tales as a test of power, and enforced at Taos as punishment; domiciliary visits are paid by ceremonial personages to collect "alms" or food[57] (some of these collectors, Aztec and Pueblo, wear garlands of flowers); an anti-sunwise ceremonial circuit is observed;[58] there are rites of running,[59] asperging,[60] including sprinkling by mouth, and of divination by peering into a bowl of water;[61] birds are observed as omens.[62] The time it takes to kindle new fire is another common omen. In both cultures there are images of the gods, permanent or temporary.[63] The Aztec made images of the sacred mountains as the Hopi and Keres appear to do.[64] The Aztec "tabernacle of painted boards for the god's image" may be compared with the painted slat altar of the Pueblo, or possibly with the painted roof shrine of Zuñi Shalako houses. Confession "to escape wordly punishment" was an Aztec practice of which the nature was puzzling to the Catholic friar,[65] just as it is puzzling to us after a Zuñi witch has confessed, punishment does not always follow. Confession is sometimes all that the war chiefs wish.

Road-guarding by snakes is a conception that finds expression in both cultures. Stone figurines of snakes are on the Hopi war chief's altar and the stone coils in Hopi trail-side shrines probably represent snakes. Snakes, also clashing mountains, have to be braved by the hero in Pueblo folktales, and by the Aztec who dies and journeys to another world. For this journey the deceased Aztec is given credentials of paper,[66] the deceased Pueblo, credentials of feather.

Aztec traders, traveling men, carried walking sticks or canes, solid light black canes, which they would tie in a bundle and venerate as the image of their god with food, flowers, and incense.[67] On returning from the extraordinary trips they made, the cane was placed in the calpulli or "district church" and later in the house shrine, where before eating the merchant offered it food. We may compare the crook sticks which are placed on Hopi altars to represent the deceased members of the society, and the crook sticks in the prayer-stick bundles, as well as the canes of the Zuñi and Isleta war chiefs. "Black cane old man" is the name used in referring to one of the Isleta war chiefs. We recall that the Pueblo canes of office are sprinkled with meal or with "holy water" and have a distinctly fetishistic character. They are placed on the altar. The Pueblos have always asserted that the war chief canes "came up with them" i.e. anteceded the Lincoln or Spanish canes or *varas*; Sahagún's account of the Aztec canes, not only the canes of the merchants but of the war chief stick,[68] seems to corroborate this tradition. I surmise that we have not only in New Mexico, but throughout old Mexico,[69] an exceedingly interesting instance of acculturation between Spanish *vara* and the walking-stick of the Aztec merchant guild and the big stick of the Aztec war chief.

The Aztec seem to have used "gum paper" very much as the Pueblo use prayer feathers. Gum paper was tied to canes and placed around the images of the gods, as feathers tied to canes, i.e. prayer sticks are bundled at Zuñi around the war god images. The Aztec hung gum paper around the neck of an image, just as the Hopi hang prayer feathers. Miniature arrows and "torches," i.e. sticks of candlewood, were placed by the Aztec on graves. We are reminded of the miniature arrows (and bows) made at Zuñi for the war gods and of the prayer-stick bundles deposited for the dead. In connection with the ritual for the dead the Aztec also made a feather-stick or cane, making small bundles of white feathers of the heron, tying two and two together and gathering the threads of these bundles and fastening them to the cornstalk cane. These Pueblo-like "prayer sticks" were carried to a stone pile where, according to a non-Pueblo pattern, they were burned.[70] The Aztec attached feathers to the tips of feathers[71] as do the Pueblo, and in both cultures feather down is used in ritual. The crook stick of Quetzalcoatl[72] and the befeathered stick of the impersonator of the salt goddess[73] remind us of the ritual staff of the Kachinas; and the ritual shields of the Aztec remind us of the shields used by the Hopi impersonators of the gods in the winter solstice ceremony.[74]

Here I cannot forbear remarking that the Hopi use of clan designs on the backs of racers, their petrographs of Kachina masks and probably other petrographs, and certain conventional designs for rain, clouds, and lightning are not very far removed from Aztec picture-writing. To explain to me what my newly acquired Hopi name meant my "father" drew me the cumulus cloud and falling rain "glyph" familiar in all the Pueblos. Had the Hopi wanted to make historical records of persons or periods or tribute they would have produced in style something much closer to Aztec glyphs than let us say the historical records of the Plains tribes.

Our list of Aztec-Pueblo ritual similarities is impressive. It might be even more so could we get from Sahagún a better impression of how the Aztec rites were weighted, how much, how frequently, they occurred. But Sahagún of course was not looking for ritual patterns; a single reference to the strewing of cornmeal or to the ceremonial circuit suffices. Nevertheless, from his particulars, which are given for the most part very objectively, we get a general impression of Aztec ritual, blood sacrifice always apart, and I may add rites of intoxication, as strikingly similar to Pueblo ritual. Even when details vary, their general character appears the same, highly conventionalized and without patent explanation. Compare the "game" of the priests who after circling the fire holding hands run down the temple steps and, letting go of each other's hands almost forcibly, fall headlong or on one side;[75] compare this with Koyemshi ritual "play." The arrow-shooting at a maguey leaf during the ceremonial of the fourteenth month[76] also recalls the ritual games of the western Pueblos. Compare the account of the rite in which the Aztec rain priest touches with a small hook four small balls of the stone called chalchivites, making each time a motion as if to withdraw his hand, then turning around and then again touching one of the four pellets, concluding with sprinkling incense and rattling a board with jingles, compare this with the Hopi rite of "casting down greasewood" at the conclusion of Niman, the farewell Kachina ceremony. The fourfold feint occurs in both rites, but that is not the point of my comparison; rather is it the general character of the two rituals, their precise, elaborate, and yet apparently meaningless character. Either ritual might be called Aztec or Pueblo, and apart from the accidental traits one would not recognize the substitution.

Now let us note a few ceremonial fragments which may be specifically compared. The new fire, drill-made, is carried out from the temple of the Aztec fire god[77] as it is carried out from the Hopi kiva where ritual has been performed for Masawa, god of fire. Like the Aztec "old men," the Hopi chiefs throw their offerings into the fire. In both cultures this ritual is performed at a ceremony which features tribal initiation, and as we shall note again, this ceremony was one of those annual ceremonies which among both Hopi and Aztec were performed more elaborately every four years. For both cultures it happens to be the last ceremony of the year. At Zuñi new fire is made at the New Year or winter solstice ceremony. At the Aztec and Hopi ceremony, initiates are carried on the backs of their "god-fathers" (as they are also carried at Zuñi initiation, part of which is performed also at the final ceremony of the Zuñi year). The Hopi initiation occurs in the same kiva in which the new fire is made. In both the Aztec and Hopi ceremony there is a special dance by the "lords" or "old men" (Wöwöchimtu).

The last five days of the Aztec year were called "idle" days; they did not work during these days because they were considered unlucky, and they refrained from quarreling.[78] Refraining from quarreling at set ceremonial times has a decidedly Pueblo ring; and in Pueblo terms these idle days would be called "staying still," taboo periods found at Zuñi, at Isleta, and at Taos. The concept of the dangerous moon, December, among the Hopi, is probably an expression of a similar way of thinking.

In what appears to be an early harvest ceremony among the Aztec, ears of corn were sprinkled with oil, wrapped in "paper" and bundled on the back of virgins to be carried in procession to the temple of the corn god and the goddess of sustenance (food plants). This was the seed corn.[79] Compare the baskets of seed corn carried in procession by the Hopi maidens and youths in the Powamu ceremony. It is called woman's corn and is supposed to yield very abundantly.[80]

At this Aztec harvest ceremony as well as at other ceremonies men and boys make domiciliary calls and are given food.[81] We recall the house-to-house visitation by the Hopi meal gatherers[82] and by the Natashka masks, and food-collecting by the Taos Black Eyes or by the Zuñi Koyemshi, and the giving of food to dance groups who go from house to house at various fiestas throughout the eastern pueblos. Some of this ritual visitation is indubitably Catholic custom, e.g., the visits by the boys on All Souls, the day of the dead, at Zuñi; but with the Aztec practices in mind the whole complex of visitation must be considered from the point of view of acculturation.

Pole-climbing is probably another acculturative matter. The Aztec climbed the ceremonial pole by ropes,[83] as I have seen it done by the Zapotecas who also grease the pole. At San Ildefonso and at Taos the pole or tree is not greased. Possibly greasing is a European feature. Scrambling for the things thrown down from the top might appear to be European—it is not done by the Pueblo—were it not a marked trait in the Aztec pole-climb. Curiously enough there is no record of pole-climbing among the western pueblos.

Ducking in water for ritual negligence was an Aztec practice,[84] as it is today at Isleta,[85] at Laguna,[86] and at Taos. Little Zuñi boys are sometimes taken to the river as a disciplinary measure by Atoshe Kachina and a Koyemshi.

In the fourteenth month of the Aztec calendar, in November, pre-liminary to festival in honor of the Otomi war god, there was held a cere-monial hunt, a surround,[87] which may be compared with the communal hunts held before ceremonies by the Pueblo.

The winding in and out dance by two women and a man or two men and a woman in an Aztec war dance[88] is suggestive of the Keresan war dance. In the Zuñi scalp ceremony the scalp-taker, his "older brother," and others come dancing into the court. Although details vary, I am strongly reminded of the general picture in reading Sahagún's accounts of the Aztec warriors who dance in procession with their captives. In fact the entire Zuñi celebration if described in Sahagún's terms would read curiously like an Aztec ceremonial.

In an Aztec rain dance held every eight years, snakes and frogs were swallowed alive, men swallowing them as they danced.[89] In the Hopi snake ceremony snakes are held in the mouth, and there is a tradition that formerly the snakes were swallowed.[90] Possibly the clever juggling feats with live snakes which Espejo reported at Acoma included some such performance, for between the Hopi and the early Keresan snake ceremonies there were undoubtedly associations.[91]

There are in Sahagún a few references to clowning or burlesque, which is so prominent a trait in Pueblo ceremonialism and which is found throughout modern Mexico in connection with folk dances. The most striking Aztec instance occurs in rain god ceremonial after the lake sacrifice of human hearts, precious stones, and ritual paper: "One of the priests took an incense burner and, acting like a poltroon (or even fool), placed on it four papers . . . set fire to them and make the motion of offertory, while they were burning."[92] This appears to be a burlesque of a most sacred rite, quite in the Pueblo manner. Other instances of Aztec clowning also suggest Pueblo parallels. On top of the Aztec temple where the pole was climbed danced a buffoon dressed like a squirrel.[93] The dance on the roof tops by the Zuñi Koyemshi is referred to as a squirrel performance. In the Aztec rain ceremony of every eight years there were impersonations of "poor people," wood-carriers and peddlers, and sick persons, which remind us of the improvised comedians of the Hopi called Piṗtüyakyamû.[94]

It was the Aztec belief that in this rain ceremony

> all the gods were dancing, and therefore the dancers were dressed in diverse fancy costumes, some impersonated birds, others different animals; some represented the bird called "tzinitzcan," others butterflies, some dressed like drones, others like flies, still others like beetles.[95]

This certainly sounds very much like Kachina dancing, without masks. The Pueblo, by the way, have a bee Kachina.

In another Aztec ceremony there is mention of a "frightful mask"[96] taking part in a sham battle between the priests (the mask is on their side) and the young townsmen or warriors. It reminds us of the fight with the Kachina performed at Acoma,[97] which has an extraordinarily bloody character for a Pueblo ceremony. Through blood-filled bladders the Kachina impersonations appear to meet a bloody death. Another expression of killing the god is met in the Hopi dramatizations of killing Masaúwüh.[98]

In the Zuñi ceremony of Ololowiskya, which at Laguna opens the hunting season, there is not only a general Aztec character but particular resemblances—impersonation, flute or trumpet playing, and a form of eating the god—balls of meal which has been ground by Kachina maids and moistened with the make-believe urine of the Kachina impersonation are given to the lookers-on.[99]

So much for parallels in ceremonial. With one surprising exception it has been out of the question to equate larger ceremonial complexes, i.e. ceremonies, or ceremonial calendars. Ceremonies and ceremonial calendars differ very widely even among the Pueblo. They must have differed very widely also among the Nahuatl-speaking peoples and even among the Aztec towns, a matter that Sahagún merely hints at in referring to distinctive divinities in different localities.

The exception is the Koko awia or Shalako of Zuñi and the ceremony of the Aztec twelfth month, Teotleco. Here there are so many points of resemblance in the ceremonial complex that some equation has to be made. In both Zuñi and Nahuatl the name of the ceremony refers to the arrival of the gods who are "said to have gone to other parts."[100] The first god to arrive in both ceremonies is a "bachelor" or virgin god. (Because of his virginity he walks faster, say the Aztec. The older gods arrive the following day. The Hopi refer to their Ahulani Kachina as moving slowly because he is such an old, old Kachina.)[101] The Aztec made a mound of corn (?meal) which was watched overnight by the head priest to see when the gods made a footprint in it in token of arrival.[102] The Zuñi make two mounds of sand covered with meal which is also watched for omens,[103] and, possibly, for the coming of the gods because a "road" of meal leads to the mounds. Should a Shalako impersonator fall in the running ritual he would be exorcised (or punished as Sahagún would say). Running ritual and a taboo against stumbling or falling[104] are Aztec traits. In the Aztec ceremony there is a midnight drinking party, which was not uncommon in other ceremonials. In the Zuñi ceremony there is also a midnight feast, which is uncommon, in fact unique, in Zuñi ceremonialism, and, curiously enough, before prohibition enforcement there was much drinking this night, nonritualistic drinking, but drinking which would not have been tolerated at other ceremonies. The Aztec made a fire around which danced "certain young men disguised as monsters." When Shulawitsi comes in in the Zuñi ceremony he kindles several large bonfires at which their dance is performed by the Sayatasha group. Their horned masks might be described as monsters better than the single figure described by Sahagún as a man with face painted black and white, with a switch of long hair and feathers and a crown on his head and with feathers and a dried rabbit on his back. The Aztec fires were for human sacrifice; the Zuñi fires are "to feed the clouds." One of the Aztec gods was the fire god; the Zuñi virgin god is the so-called little fire god.

The Hopi also celebrate Shalako, as a loan ceremony from Zuñi, although there is said to be a "native" Hopi Shalako ceremony. One element of the Shalako, the coming and going of the gods, is expressed in other Hopi ceremonies, in the Niman or farewell Kachina ceremony and in the Kachina return dances.

Another Aztec trait that is expressed in Shalako, and, as noted, in the horned water serpent ceremony of the Hopi and in Hopi Kachina dances, is the entertainment of the god in private houses, by nonsacerdotalists. The god is offered a celebration.[105] There are still other Aztec traits we may note in Shalako. The impersonators of the gods serve for a year, and some of them are referred to during their services by their god's name. For example, the impersonator of Sayatasha will be called Sayatasha in the daily familiar speech of the townspeople.[106] When the Shalako masks leave town it is said they are struck at and thrown down, which is suggestive of the killing of the god. This ritual no white has ever been allowed to see. The Shalako are or were thought of as warriors (in Aztec terms, prisoners of war), for in their belts they carry war clubs. The attachment of feathers to the blanket costume of the Shalako, a very elaborate arrangement on First Mesa, suggests an Aztec technique. Finally we note that one of the Shalako day counts is by ten, an Aztec and *not* a Pueblo count.

There are a few general calendrical similarities as well as dissimilarities which we may note, particularly between Hopi and Aztec. The Hopi like the other Pueblo have a calendar based on both lunar and solar observations, the moon's phases being observed, and sunrise and sunset being noted by points on the horizon for a solstitial horizon calendar. Lunar and solar observations are inferred by Spinden to have been the basis of the early Maya calendar and so presumably of the Aztec calendar. But the Maya-Aztec developed a day-count never achieved by the Pueblos, who "count their days" in relation to sun or moon, but for short ceremonial periods only. The Zuñi tally string for Shalako, a count of forty-nine days, is the longest count achieved. In their historic period the Maya and Aztec disregarded the moon's phases, having eighteen months of twenty days each, a purely arbitrary arrangement for the sequence of their ceremonies, a ceremony being assigned to each twenty-day period. In Mexican and Pueblo cultures alike the divisions of the year, however they were made, were for the determination of ceremonies, for the sake of the ceremonial sequence.

If the length of a ceremony is counted from the time of its announcement, the duration of a Hopi ceremony, and of some Zuñi ceremonies, corresponds to the duration of Aztec ceremonies, only the Pueblo use a multiple of four, their favored numeral, and the Aztec, a multiple of five, their favored numeral.[107] This variation results in a sixteen-day period for the Pueblo and in a twenty-day period for the Aztec. Possibly we have a clue here for the original substitution by the Mexicans for the twenty-day month for the lunar month. We may note that the Hopi name the days in their ceremonial day-count. The names refer to the stereotype conduct of the day, just as the Aztec called the day after their interval rain god fast molpololo, meaning "they ate other things with the bread."[108]

The performance of ceremonies in long or short forms is an Aztec-Hopi parallel, as is also the lapse of years between the performance of certain ceremonies. The Aztec had a year count to which the Pueblos are indifferent, but in timing interval ceremonies it is possible that "every eight years" or "every four years" was used as loosely by the Aztec as is the "every four years" of the Hopi-Zuñi calendars. The Pueblo are realists: they hold an initiation when there are enough individuals to initiate, or they make a rain pilgrimage in time of drought or delay a ceremony if the crops are maturing slowly. The Aztec were probably realists also, and Sahagún's calendar may be overstereotyped.

A few more words on comparisons of pantheon. Not only the Pueblo water gods but the Corn Mothers, possibly Muyingwa, the Hopi male corn god, Salt Old Woman, possibly Masawa, the Hopi god of fire and of death, possibly the twin war gods, are to be recognized in the Aztec pantheon.[109] The description of Centeotl would serve for Iatiku of the Keresan curing society—mother of the gods, heart of the earth, our grandmother, the goddess of the doctors. Corn mothers or maidens figure among all the Pueblo, but only the Hopi have a male corn god, Muyingwa. Muyingwa is impersonated by a "priest" in the Powamu ceremony[110] quite in the Aztec mode. The banishment or departure of the salt goddess is plainly a variant of the Pueblo tale of Salt Woman who takes offense at the way she is treated and makes off in a huff to distant parts. But for the priggishness of Sahagún or of his early editors the variant would be even closer, I surmise. He refers to the incident merely as "a certain misfortune (disgrace)." The Hopi god Masawa is unique in the general Pueblo pantheon; he is almost a high god with the formidable character of an Aztec god. Even Bear is afraid of Masawa who is associated with bloody rituals. Besides Masawa, the Hopi have the twin or brother war gods of the other Pueblo, who remind us of the Aztec war god and his "favorite" or "sub-captain." Like the Pueblo war gods these two, Vitzilopuchtli and Paynal, were impersonated and to Vitzilopuchtli a magical impregnation story attaches, in the Pueblo style.[111]

The Mexicans believed that the early gods died or withdrew below ground, becoming stone.[112] Elements of this tradition may be recognized among the Pueblo. That some of the gods or personages of the early days became stone is a general Pueblo belief,[113] and the Hopi idea that the gods emerge from the sipapu of the kiva would seem to be related to the Mexican idea of the gods' retirement below their temples.

The social organization of the Aztec in so far as it was based on the dedication of sons by their parents to various groups is paralleled among the Pueblos. After birth a Zuñi or Acoma or Taos boy is given to one of the kivas, the prime function of which is now ceremonial dancing, but which once, I think, had war functions; a Hopi boy is given to one of the four tribal societies of which two are or were warrior groups; even where the hereditary moiety prevails, as among the Tewa, dedication or vowing of children to special groups occurs. Social classification by wealth and birth was far more marked among the Aztec than among the Pueblo, although I think the Spanish chroniclers exaggerated by the light of their own culture, and that the classification was nearer to that prevailing today at Zuñi, where poor people are those who belong to no ceremonial groups and the rich those possessed of ritual paraphernalia and society membership. Indeed only in this way does Sahagún's account of the training of Aztec youth make sense. He states that the education of the boys was divided into two distinct classes, for sons of commoners and for sons of chiefs or old men, which can only mean priests (or doctors) who, as Sahagún himself states, held office irrespective of high lineage or wealth. The high priests were chosen for fitness "even if they should be of very low birth and of very lowly and poor parents."[114] How then were they ever entered in the school for chiefs and "old men" unless they were the sons of the "old men" and unless these might be lowly and poor; that is lowly and poor from Sahagún's point of view? It is a very confused statement, due, I think, to the confusion of two quite different cultural points of view. The account clears up somewhat if the difference in education and schools is thought of primarily as functional; the telpuchcalli was for military and political training, the calmecac, for sacerdotal training. In the four Hopi tribal societies there is something of the same kind of differentiation: the Agaves and Horns are scouts, patrols, errand men; the Singers and Wöwöchim are possessed of curing ritual and of certain songs and dances. Throughout the Pueblos a similar differentiation is indicated: ceremonialists (singers), those with military or police functions, and dancers, or the younger men at large.

By Sahagún's account of the training in the telpuchcalli we are reminded of much in the life of the kivas of the western pueblos—dance practice at night, fetching firewood (compare the initiation of the Hopi youths),[115] sleeping in their ceremonial building, but eating at home, communal service, military service. Military service is still indicated among the Hopi Agave and Horn societies and as I have said the kiva groupings of men at Zuñi and elsewhere may once have been military groupings, the soldiering having lapsed and the dancing developed. Incidentally I note that the Aztec fighting men wore "tufts of white plumes in their hair" and tied balls of cotton yarn to their wrists,[116] as Pueblo Kachina dancers do today.

The system of communal service which prevailed among the Aztec and probably among many other Mexican peoples was undoubtedly taken over by the Spaniards to combine with their own system of town government and to develop into the political system which prevails today in all the smaller towns of Mexico as well as among the Pueblos. Among them all one characteristic Indian character tends to survive, the blending of judicial and executive offices.[117]

Of family or kinship organization Sahagún tells us little or nothing. As yet there is no evidence anywhere in Mexico, either pre-Conquest or modern Mexico, for any organization other than the compound family group, with bilateral descent and some emphasis upon inheritance through the father of property, position, and functions. Among several peoples kinship terms are applied in the characteristic Indian classificatory way, classification by generation, but I doubt if this practice alone is evidence for the existence of kinship groups which are not remembered as actually related by blood. Among the Pueblos, Taos has the classificatory system and Taos is clanless. There is a tendency toward paternal inheritance among its paramount chieftaincies. The moieties of the Tewa and the kiva organization of Tewa and Keres are based on paternal descent. Neither to the eastern pueblos nor to old Mexico can the western pueblos look for affiliations in their system of exogamous maternal clans.

The godfather or ceremonial father or sponsor the Aztec and all the Pueblos, western as well as eastern, have in common. The combination of Indian sponsor and Spanish *padrino* is one of the most interesting of all the expressions of acculturation in the social organization of hispanicized Indians. The Spanish *compadre* system undoubtedly fitted into the Indian sponsor (and kinship) system.

Between Aztec and Spaniards there were favorable conditions for acculturation in attitudes toward days of birth, toward patron saints' days, and days favorable for birth in the Aztec calendar—conditions which did not occur between Pueblo and Spaniards, for the Pueblo calendar, unlike the Aztec and the Augustan, does not allow for prognostication for every day of the year. However, in one or two cases the Pueblo attaches importance to the time of conception and relates it quite in the Aztec manner to the god's ceremony. Children conceived during the Zuñi scalp ceremony are under the protection of the gods of war and are especially strong, becoming sturdy men and women.[118] Somewhat similarly Laguna children conceived on Christmas eve were called the saint's children, at least according to a Zuñi visitor who ridiculed the custom, seeing no relation, of course, between it and Zuñi custom.

Among the Aztec there are pregnancy taboos, on both parents, which are of the same type as Pueblo pregnancy taboos. Compare the Aztec belief, that a pregnant woman should not see a man hanged lest the child be marked, with the Pueblo belief that a pregnant woman should not see certain masks lest the child be born blind or with a twisted mouth. The Pueblo belief that the child will have a harelip if his mother is exposed to a lunar eclipse is also Aztec belief. In both cultures the prophylaxis is the same, carrying a stone knife in the dress. The Pueblo carry other things too, but in Pueblo circles an arrowpoint is the most usual talisman against supernatural danger. Aztec and Pueblo have both a rite of presenting the infant to the sun at sunrise.[119] The Aztec kept a fire burning for the first four days after the birth,[120] just as some of the Pueblo do. Asking for the bride and asking repeatedly was Aztec custom,[121] as it is Isleta custom. The Hopi marriage procession recalls the Aztec marriage procession. Four days after a death heads are washed, by Aztec[122] and Pueblo. The spirit of the deceased has lingered for four days. The spirit transforms into a bird of fine hues,[123] just as at Zuñi and Santo Domingo[124] the spirit may transform into a duck.

*NOTES*
*INDEX*

# NOTES

## PART 1

### 1 The Mesoamerican Southwest

1. Basil C. Hedrick, J. Charles Kelley, and Carroll L. Riley, eds., *The North Mexican Frontier* (Carbondale, 1971).
2. Basil C. Hedrick, J. Charles Kelley, and Carroll L. Riley, eds., *The Classic Southwest* (Carbondale, 1973).
3. Edwin N. Ferdon, *A Trial Survey of Mexican-Southwestern Architectural Parallels*, Monographs of the School of American Research, no. 27 (Santa Fe, 1955).
4. Jesse D. Jennings et al., "The American Southwest: A Problem in Cultural Isolation," in *Seminars in Archaeology: 1955* (Salt Lake City, 1956), pp. 59–129.
5. William W. Wosley, "The Hohokam Platform Mound at the Gatlin Site, Gila Bend, Arizona," *American Antiquity* 26 (1960): 244–62.
6. Charles C. DiPeso, "Archaeology and Ethnohistory of the Northern Sierra," in *Handbook of Middle American Indians* (Austin, 1966), 4: 21–22; Charles C. DiPeso, "Casas Grandes and the Gran Chichimeca," *El Palacio* 74 (1968): 45–61.
7. Albert H. Schroeder, "Unregulated Diffusion from Mexico into the Southwest Prior to A.D. 700," *American Antiquity* 30 (1965): 297–309; Albert H. Schroeder, "Pattern Diffusion from Mexico into the Southwest after A.D. 600," *American Antiquity* 31 (1966): pp. 683–704.
8. Donald D. Brand, "Aboriginal Trade Routes for Sea Shells in The Southwest," *Yearbook of the Association of Pacific Coast Geographers* 4 (1938): pp. 3–10, reprinted in Hedrick, Kelley, Riley, 1973, pp. 92–101.
9. Alvar Nuñez Cabeza de Vaca, *Naufragios* (Mexico City, 1944), p. 62.
10. Carroll L. Riley, "Blacks in the Early Southwest," *Ethnohistory* 19 (1972): 247–60.
11. Carroll L. Riley, "Early Spanish-Indian Communication in the Greater Southwest," *New Mexico Historical Review* 46 (1971): 285–314.

Joaquín F. Pacheco and Francisco Cárdenas, *Colección de documentos ineditos relativos al descubrimiento conquista y organización de las posesiones españoles de américa y oceania* (DII), vol. 3 (Madrid, 1865).

12. George P. Hammond and Agapito Rey, *Narratives of the Coronado Expedition 1540–1542* (Albuquerque, 1940); George P. Hammond and Agapito Rey, *The Rediscovery of New Mexico 1580–1594,* (Albuquerque, 1966).
13. Riley 1971; Hammond and Rey 1940.
14. Riley 1971, p. 304; Carroll L. Riley, "Mexican Indians in the Sixteenth Century Southwestern U.S.A.," *América Indígena* (n.d. [in press]).
15. Riley 1971, pp. 304–6.
16. Riley (n.d.).
17. J. Charles Kelley, "Mesoamerica and the Southwest United States," in *Handbook of Middle American Indians* (Austin, 1966), 4: 95–110; DiPeso 1968; Carroll L. Riley, "Color Direction Symbolism in the Greater Southwest," *América Indígena* 23 (1963): 49–60.
18. Riley 1972.
19. Charles Lumholtz, *Unknown Mexico* (New York, 1902), p. 368.

**PART 2**

**Introduction**

1. Charles C. DiPeso, "Archaeology and Ethnohistory of the Northern Sierra," in *Handbook of Middle American Indians* (Austin, 1966), 4: 20–21.
2. Ralph L. Beals, *The Aboriginal Culture of the Cáhita Indians* (Berkeley and Los Angeles), p. 34.
3. Paul S. Martin, George I. Quimby, and Donald Collier, *Indians Before Columbus* (Chicago, 1947), pp. 174–75.
4. Edwin N. Ferdon, Jr., "The Hohokam 'Ball Court' An Alternate View of Its Function," *Kiva,* 33 (1967): 8–12.
5. Jesse D. Jennings, *Prehistory of North America* (New York, 1968), p. 262.
6. J. Charles Kelley, "Mesoamerica and the Southwest United States," in *Handbook of the Middle American Indians* (Austin, 1966), 4: 95–110.

**2 Guayule**

1. Investigated by G. R. Endlich *in* F. Altamirano, *Datos para la historia y explotación del "Guayule,"* Boletín de la Secretaría de Fomento de México (Segunda época), vol. 5 (1906), pp. 1098–1123. The Altamirano paper is a composite, and contains a translation of a paper by G. R. Endlich in *Tropenflanzer* 9 (1905): 223, 11 (1907): 449; English translation, *India Rubber World* (1905).
2. The name is also applied to *Crysactinia mexicana* Gray, and more recently also to *Euphorbia misera,* materials of which was sent to Dr. J.

N. Rose, of the U.S. National Herbarium, from southern California, on the supposition that it contained rubber.

3. The female guayule.

4. From the Nahuatl *xihuitl*, weed. This spelling is given by Endlich. "Jihuite" is given in Zacatecas. "Gihuete" occurs in a legal instrument drawn up at Matamoras, Coahuila, under date of March 9, 1905, in which also "hule" is given as designating guayule.

5. Endlich 1906.

6. According to Juan Fritz, see Endlich 1906.

7. H. Jumelle, *Les plantes a caoutchouc et à gutta* (Paris, 1903), quotes these authors at length.

8. According to Juan Robles, whose duty it was, in 1856, to weigh the shrub as it came into the fundición at Cedros, guayule was paid for at the rate of 18 centavos per carga (6 arrobas = 70 kilos), or about 17 pounds for 1 cent (gold)! The women on Cedros burned guayule in their bread ovens as late as 1894 (see R. G. Fleming [not cited]). Guayule shrub now fetches 150 pesos the ton.

#### 4  A Pre-Spanish Rubber Ball from Arizona

1. A preliminary notice of this ball, by Charles Amsden, will be found in *Masterkey* 10 (1936): 7–8.

2. Gila Pueblo, Globe, Arizona.

3. F. Blom, *The Maya Ball-Game Pok-ta-pok*, Middle American Research Series, Publication no. 4, Middle American Papers (New Orleans, 1932), pp. 487–527.

4. F. E. Lloyd, *Guayule: A Rubber Plant of the Chihuahuan Desert*, Carnegie Institution of Washington, Publication no. 193 (Washington, D.C., 1911), p. 6.

5. The lack of house remains on the surface is easily understood, as during the period represented by the find, houses were semisubterranean and their presence is not manifested by surface features.

6. Gonzalo Fernández de Oviedo y Valdes, *Historia general y natural de las Indias* . . . 1 (Madrid, 1851): 165, describes the balls of Central America as manufactured "out of roots of trees and herbs and juices and mixtures of wax and pitch."

7. By letter, January 8, 1936.

8. "In the Codex Mendoza we see that twenty-two towns located on the Gulf Coast between northern Oaxaca and the Gulf paid 16,000 rubber balls as tribute every year to the court of Mexico," Blom 1932, p. 498.

#### PART 3

#### Introduction

1. Adolph F. Bandelier, "Final Report of Investigations among the Indians of the Southwestern United States, 2 parts," Papers of the Archaeological

Institute of America, American Series, 3 and 4 (Cambridge, Mass., 1890 and 1892).

2. Charles H. Lange and Carroll L. Riley, eds., *The Southwestern Journals of Adolph F. Bandelier, 1883–1884* (Albuquerque, 1970), pp. 219–327.

3. Ernest J. Burrus, S.J., *A History of the Southwest by Adolph F. Bandelier*, vol. 1, Supplement, Jesuit Historical Institute, Sources and Studies for the History of the Americas, vol. 7 (Rome, 1969), p. 499.

4. Charles H. Lange, Carroll L. Riley and Elizabeth M. Lange, eds., *The Southwestern Journal of Adolph F. Bandelier, 1885–1888* (Albuquerque, forthcoming).

5. Mariano Cuevas, *Historia de los Descubrimientos Antiguos y Modernos de la Nueva España, escrito por, Baltasar de Obregón* (Mexico, 1924).

6. Carroll L. Riley, "Adolph Bandelier—The Mexican Years," *América Indígena* 28 (1968): 431; Charles H. Lange and Carroll L. Riley, eds., *The Southwestern Journals of Adolph F. Bandelier, 1880–1882* (Albuquerque, 1966), pp. 13–16.

7. Charles C. Dipeso, "Archaeology and Ethnohistory of the Northern Sierra," in *Handbook of Middle American Indians* (Austin, 1966), 4: 21–22.

**PART 4**

**Introduction**

1. Charles H. Lange and Carroll L. Riley, eds., *The Southwestern Journals of Adolph F. Bandelier, 1880–1882* (Albuquerque, 1966), pp. 23–26.

2. Charles H. Lange and Carroll L. Riley, *The Southwestern Journals of Adolph F. Bandelier, 1883–1884* (Albuquerque, 1970), pp. 47, 50.

3. Adolph F. Bandelier, "Final Report of Investigations Among the Indians of the Southwestern United States," 2 parts, Papers of the Archaeological Institute of America, American Series, 3 and 4 (Cambridge, Mass., 1890 and 1892).

4. Carl O. Sauer, "The Road to Cibola," *Ibero-Americana*, no. 3 (1932); Henry R. Wagner, "Fray Marcos de Nizza," *New Mexico Historical Review* 9 (1934): 184–227; Cleve Hallenbeck, *The Journey of Fray Marcos de Niza* (Dallas, 1949).

5. Carroll L. Riley, "Early Spanish Indian Communication in the Greater Southwest," *New Mexico Historical Review* 46 (1971): 285–314.

6. Adolph F. Bandelier, "Fray Juan de Padilla, the First Catholic Missionary and Martyr in Eastern Kansas, 1542," *American Catholic Quarterly Review* 15 (1890): 551–65; reprinted in *The Classic Southwest*, ed. Basil C. Hedrick, J. Charles Kelley, Carroll L. Riley (Carbondale, 1973), pp. 51–63.

7. Sauer 1932, pp. 22–24.

### The Discovery of New Mexico by Fray Marcos of Nizza

1. [*Ed. note.* These four men were Alvar Núñez Cabeza de Vaca, Andrés Dorantes, Alonso de Castillo Maldonado, and Esteban (Bandelier's Estevan) a black slave of Dorantes.]
2. The expedition of Nuño Beltrán de Guzmán, successor to Cortéz, began in 1529. It cannot have been any other than the Colorado, for the Spaniards had already discovered the Yaqui then.
3. For a modern English translation of these instructions see Hammond, George P. and Agapito Rey, *Narratives of the Coronado Expedition, 1540–42* (Albuquerque, 1940), pp. 58–61.
4. [Marcos de Niza] says that Vacapa was 40 leagues (108 miles) from the sea. Compare on the location of the place the map of Father Eusebio Kino (Kunhoe) in Father Joseph Stöcklein, *Der neue Weltott von denen missionariis der Gesellschaft Jesu aus beyden Indien*, 2d ed., vol. 1 (Grätz, 1728); "Noticia breve de le expedición militar de Sonora y Sinaloa," *Documentos para la Historia de Méjico*, 4th ser., vol 1, chap. 8; "Trip of Father Juan María de Salvatierra and F. Eusebio Kino, twenty-seventh of February to sixteenth of April, 1701," p. 327, no title [MS provenience unknown]. Vacapa is placed thirty leagues N.W. and six leagues N. and N.E. of Caborca, and the writer says: "y parece es por lo que pasó el ejército de Francisco Vásquez Coronado el año de 1540." He bases his opinion on the name and on the distance from the coast. The name proves nothing. Pima names, as well as Opata names, occur in Sonora and Arizona sometimes half a dozen times. I know, from personal visit, two "Bamori," two "Bamochi," two "Nacori," etc., etc. Neither is the distance a criterion. Matape is not one hundred and twenty miles from the seashore. It is an old mission, having been founded among the "Eudeves" (a dialect of the Opata) in 1629. Manuel Orozco y Berra, *Geografía de las lenguas y carta etnografia de Mexico* (Mexico, 1864), p. 344. The distance from Vacapa to the "desert" (112 leagues or 312 miles) points strongly to Matape, so does the description of the country. But there is still another proof in favor of Matape. While sojourning along the coast, inhabitants of two islands, a larger and a smaller one, came to see the father, and they also visited him while at Vacapa (p. 262). The "Isla del Tiburón" and "del Angel de la Guardia" lie almost in the parallel of Matape, whereas from the Bacapa of Kino they are at least two hundred miles due *south*. It is not likely that Fray Marcos, having had intercourse with the Indians of these islands, would have waited until he was far to the north to send his people back after them.
5. The "Guaymas" were a branch of the "Seris" and spoke a dialect of their language. The Seris occupied, in the early part of the seventeenth century, the coast of Sonora from Guaymas north. Their savagery and ferocity are well known. Compare Andres Pérez de Ribas, *Historia de*

*los triumphos de nuestra santa fee . . . Madrid* (1645), lib. 6, chap. 1, p. 359: "es sobremanero bozal, sin pueblos, sin casas, ni sementeras." See also lib. 6, chap. 18, p. 392.

6. It is the only valley in Sonora that could correspond to the description of Fray Marcos. I have examined it closely, under the auspices of the archaeological institute, as far south of the line as Babiácora and am convinced that the friar took this route. This is further proven by the well-established fact that, the next year, he led Coronado and his forces up the Sonora Valley. Castañeda says that when Coronado went from Culiacán to Cibola (by way of Sonora) all the Indians on the line of march knew Fray Marcos. That the Opatas were, and still are, the inhabitants of the valley is a well-known fact which requires no further proof. [*Ed. note.* More recent work on Marcos route suggests that he may not have gone up the Sonora River valley. For discussions of various sections of the Marcos Route see George J. Undreiner, "Fray Marcos de Niza and his Journey to Cibola" *The Americas* 3 (1947): 415–86; Albert H. Schroeder, "Fray Marcos de Niza, Coronado, and the Yavapai," *New Mexico Historical Review* 30 (1955): 265–96; 31 (1956): 24–37; and Carroll L. Riley, "Early Spanish-Indian Communication in the Greater Southwest" *New Mexico Historical Review* 46 (1971): 289–93.]

7. The Pimas of Arizona inhabited, and still inhabit, the Gila within two hundred miles of Zuñi. They paint themselves in a striking manner. East of Matape—or rather southeast—are the lower Pima missions and the "Valley of the Hearts."

8. The ruins of any consequence begin at Los Fresnos, but they are old, and Mututicachi, about ten miles north of Bacuachi, was probably the last settlement of the Opatas along the Sonora to the northward. The village was abandoned in consequence of the Apaches. Beyond it the country was deserted until to the middle course of the San Pedro in Arizona, near Contention, a difficult stretch of fifty miles in a straight line, but of seventy at least in following water-courses.

9. "At this latitude," Marcos says, "the coast turns [to the west] and the Gulf of California terminates." This is absolutely true, though his latitude (35°) is of course wrong. It should be 32° latitude, north.

10. These names are found yet in all the maps published as late as 1657, which shows what a firm hold the nomenclature of Fray Marcos had acquired. [*Ed. note.* It is interesting that the *Benavides memorial* of 1630 retains the names in one section of the document in spite of the fact that Benavides himself had lived for several years in New Mexico. See Carroll L. Riley, "Las Casas and the Benavides Memorial of 1630" *New Mexico Historical Review* 47 (1973): 209–22.]

11. This would leave it in the neighborhood of Fort Grant.

12. The catastrophe has been often enough described.

13. In November 1539, the viceroy sent out an expedition to test the credi-

bility of Fray Marcos. The report of its commander, Melchior Díaz, is contained in the second letter of Don Antonio de Mendoza. It mentions Totonteac and fully confirms the missionary's statements. [*Ed. note.* This is not completely true. Melchior Díaz was somewhat skeptical of Marcos's claims. His report was somewhat more modest especially as regards populations. See George P. Hammond and Agapito Rey, *The Rediscovery of New Mexico, 1580–1594* (Albuquerque, 1966), pp. 157–60.]

14. Antonio de Herrera, *Historia general de los Hechos de los castellanos en las Islas y la Tierra del mar Océano* (Madrid, 1726), 2:159 says: "en la falda de un Cerro redondo." This is even more appropriate than the French translation, and applies perfectly to Caquima as seen from the south. I surveyed the Ruins in 1883, while enjoying the hospitality of Mr. Cushing. It is well situated for defense. [*Ed. note.* As a result of subsequent work it is now generally agreed that Hawikuh was the first Zuñi town approached by Esteban, (perhaps) by Marcos, and by Coronado.]

15. The father was deceived by his own experience in Peru, where the natives knew gold as gold and not simply judged by the color.

16. [*Ed. note.* This of course is sheer nonsense. Esteban clearly was the first individual of European culture to "discover" the pueblo area. See Carroll L. Riley, "Blacks in the Early Southwest" *Ethnohistory* 9 (1972): 247–60. Of course a major thrust of the present volume is to demonstrate that the Southwest Pueblo Indians had been in close trade contact with people to the south for many centuries. In the context of this book we must view the voyages of Esteban, Marcos, and Coronado as episodes in a history of contacts going back many centuries.]

## PART 5

### Introduction

1. Carroll L. Riley, "The Southern Tepehuan and Tepecano," *Handbook of Middle American Indians* (Austin, 1969), 8: 814–21; Campbell W. Pennington, *The Tepehuan of Chihuahua* (Salt Lake City, 1969).

### 8 Cultural Relations between Northern Mexico and the Southwest United States

1. Ralph L. Beals, "The Comparative Ethnology of Northern Mexico before 1750," *Ibero-Americana*, no. 2 (1932).

2. Paul Kirchhoff, "Las Tribus de la Baja California y el Libro del P. Baegert," Introduction to *Noticias de la Península Americana de California* by P. Juan Jacobo Baegert (Mexico, 1942).

3. "Arid North America" has many faults as a term. In my original draft, I hesitated to use any extension of the term "Southwest," both because of its many connotations, and because I feared extension of the word "Southwest" into any considerable part of Mexico might be considered an act of unwarranted cultural imperialism. In discussions at the con-

ference, many persons spontaneously used the term "Greater Southwest," while others fell back on the old term "Southwest," making it
clear at the same time that they considered the word to refer to southwestern North America, not merely the southwestern United States. In
revising this paper for publication, I have abandoned the term "Arid
North America" in the balance of the text and am using the term
"Greater Southwest." Neither terminology seems wholly satisfactory,
however; should the hypothesis advanced here seem worth developing,
search should be continued for a better term.

4. Although not arid, central California possesses a prolonged dry season.
The acorn substitutes for the pinyon and mesquite; utilization of grass
and other small seeds is similar in importance and techniques. On the
other hand, the arid high plains must be excluded. Culturally and bo-
tanically the plains are very different.

### 9 Relation between Mesoamerica and the Southwest

1. In this connection, it is worth observing that, on the basis of existing
data, the ceremonial systems of Aztecs and Mayas were unworkable
unless the population could attend two ceremonies at the same time. If
for the extremely numerous "priesthoods" we substitute "ceremonial
societies" on the Pueblo model and assume that only society members
took part in most of the ceremonials, the picture becomes strikingly like
that at Zuñi on a somewhat larger scale. Many other complex Aztec
features become surprisingly simplified if viewed through Pueblo-tinted
glasses.

2. I am not unaware, of course, that the Kachina cult was considerably
modified in historic times. In various papers Parsons has shown that
modification went so far as to incorporate Catholic saints into the cult
as Kachinas.

3. The picture no doubt is further complicated by local developments
which in some cases underwent fairly extensive diffusion.

### PART 7

### 11 The Butterfly in Hopi Myth and Ritual

1. The Oraibe, variant of this ceremony, described by the Rev. H. R. Voth
[probably, "The Oraibi Oagol Ceremony"], *Field Museum of Natural
History* [6 (1903): 1–46], as the Oakolti, is under the direction of other
clans, the Tuwa of Sand predominating.

2. The Badger people are said to have introduced the masked Kachina
dances among the Hopi and the shrine in which prayersticks are deposited at the dance called the farewell Kachina is called the Badger *sipapû*.

3. Walpi was founded by Bear clans; Sikyatki by Kokop; while Awatobi
and the villages on Antelope mesa are ascribed to Keres and Tewa
colonists.

4. As the Hopi have the matriarchal clan system these women may be said to have thus introduced their clans into the pueblos of their captors.
5. I have often asked the Hopi whether the people at Sikyatki and Awatobi spoke what we now call the Hopi language. One of my best informants said the Awatobi speech was Hopi but with dialectic variations, and it is instructive that a variant of the name Awatobi dates back to 1583. There is a song known to some of the old men of Walpi which is said to come from Awatobi in which many words are incomprehensible, a fact which may mean much or little as Hopi songs have many archaic words and many Keres words. The names of Tapolo and Sakeva, two chiefs of Awatobi, do not now occur on the east mesa.
6. To show the change in Zuñi symbols of the butterfly compare a picture of this insect figured in J. Walter Fewkes, "Ancient Zuñi Pottery," in *Putnam Anniversary Volume* (New York, 1909), p. 56, and numerous representations on modern Zuñi pottery. The well-known pictures of butterflies embroidered on modern Hopi wedding-blankets are closer to modern Zuñi pictures of this insect than to those of ancient Hopi or ancient Zuñi.
7. This power was regarded as magical since it was incomprehensible.
8. In a subsequent article, I will mention the places visited by the Hopi in their visits to the "Canyon" for salt, and the ceremonies when they procured this substance.
9. Later these were sold by Mr. Keam to the Berlin Museum für Völkerkünde.
10. J. Walter Fewkes, *Expedition to Arizona in 1895*, Annual Report of the Bureau of American Ethnology, no. 17, pt. 2 (1898).
11. An offering constantly made and used in Hopi ceremonies as may be seen by consulting detailed accounts of the great Hopi festivals.
12. We sometimes, as in the specimen of a food bowl from Sikyatki, find a representation of this dot, string, and attached feather at the corners of a blanket worn by a human figure.
13. J. W. Fewkes, "Minor Hopi Festivals," *American Anthropologist* 4 (1902): 506–9.
14. This is the dance called the "Hopi Harvest Dance," colored figures of which as performed at Oraibe are printed on postal cards.
15. This is commonly used as a harvest dance and is sometimes so called.
16. *Koyeamishi.*
17. J. W. Fewkes, "The New Fire Ceremony at Walpi," *American Anthropologist*, n.s. 2 (1900): 80–138.
18. These melodies were later published in Benjamin Ives Gilman, "Hopi Songs," *Journal of American Ethnology and Archaeology*, vol. 5 (1908).
19. Some of the Hano have also a Balülikon effigy.
20. Provided of course that the "ancients" who peopled compounds like Casa Grande on the Gila spoke the Pima language or some dialect of the same stock.

### PART 8

**12  The Problem of Contacts between the Southwestern United States and Mexico**

1. R. L. Beals, "The Comparative Ethnology of Northern Mexico Before 1750," *Ibero-Americana*, no. 2 (1932); R. L. Beals, "Relations Between Meso America and the Southwest," *Tercera Reunión de Mesa Redonda Sobre Problemas Antropológicos de México y Centro América* (Mexico City, 1943), pp. 245–52.

2. A. L. Kroeber, *Native Culture in the Southwest*, University of California Publications in American Archaeology and Ethnology, vol. 23 (1928), pp. 375–98.

3. S. B. Vaillant and G. C. Vaillant, "Excavations at Gualupita," Anthropological Papers of the American Museum of Natural History, vol. 35 (1934).

4. H. S. Gladwin, "Excavations at Snaketown: II. Comparisons and Theories," Medallion Papers, no. 26 (1937), pp. 15 ff.

5. C. Sauer and D. Brand, *Prehistoric Settlements of Sonora with Special Reference to Cerros de Trincheras*, University of California Publications in Geography, vol. 5 (1931), pp. 67–148; C. Sauer and D. Brand, "Aztatlán: Prehistoric Mexican Frontier on the Pacific Coast," *Ibero-Americana*, no. 1 (1932).

6. E. B. Sayles, "An Archaeological Survey of Chihuahua, Mexico," Medallion Papers, no. 22 (1936).

7. I. T. Kelly, "Excavations at Chametla, Sinaola," *Ibero-Americana*, no. 14 (1938).

8. G. F. Ekholm, "Excavations at Guasave, Sinaloa, Mexico," Anthropological Papers of the American Museum of Natural History, vol. 38 (1942).

9. E. B. Sayles, "An Archaeological Survey of Texas," Medallion Papers, no. 17 (1935).

10. E. B. Sayles and E. Anteus, "The Cochise Culture," Medallion Papers, no. 29 (1941).

11. M. J. Rogers, "Early Lithic Industries of the Lower Basin of the Colorado River and Adjacent Desert Areas," San Diego Museum Papers, no. 3 (1939).

12. D. D. Brand, "A Note on the Pre-Ceramic Man in Northern Mexico," *Tercera Reunión de Mesa Redonda Sobre Problemas Antropológicos de México y Centro América* (Mexico City, 1943), p. 164.

13. The spindle whorl at Pecos (A. V. Kidder, "The Artifacts of Pecos," Papers of the Phillips Academy Southwestern Expedition, no. 6 [1932], p. 309), and the Oaxacan carved jade found at Awatovi (J. O. Brew, "Mexican Influence upon the Indian Culture of the Southwestern United States in the Sixteenth and Seventeenth Centuries," in *The Maya and Their Neighbors* [New York, 1940], pp. 346–47]).

14. G. C. Vaillant, "Some Resemblances in the Ceramics of Central and North America," Medallion Papers, no. 12 (1932), p. 9.
15. Ibid.
16. Gladwin 1937, as incidental to a study of analogies between the Old and New Worlds.
17. The mano and metate are not considered to have arrived with corn as antecedent milling stones were extensively employed locally by food-gatherers, as in the Cochise culture. The adaptation of these to corn-grinding was a simple procedure. Had the metate come in with corn, it is likely that the legged form, early in Mexico (G. C. Vaillant, "Excavations at Zacatenco," Anthropological Papers of the American Museum of Natural History, vol. 32 (1930), pl. 7, 46; G. C. Vaillant, "Excavations at Ticoman," Anthropological Papers of the American Museum of Natural History, vol. 32 (1931), pl. 89, bottom row, no. 3) would have been represented in pre-Columbian times.
18. Beyond certain religious elements of southern complexion which doubt-less were pre-Spanish, as reasoned from modern survivals, there is little to show that the great emphasis on religious structures in Mexico affected the local groups in any way.
19. H. S. Gladwin, E. W. Haury, E. B. Sayles, and N. Gladwin, "Excavations at Snaketown: Material Culture," Medallion Papers, no. 25 (1937), pp. 36–49; C. S. Chard, "Distribution and Significance of Ball Courts in the Southwest," Papers of the Excavator's Club, vol. 1 (1941).
20. J. C. McGregor, *Winona and Ridge Ruin: Part I. Architecture and Material Culture*," Bulletin of the Museum of Northern Arizona, no. 18 (1941), pp. 83–89.
21. Gladwin, Haury, Sayles, and Gladwin 1937, pp. 163–65; G. H. Pepper, "Pueblo Bonito," Anthropological Papers of the American Museum of Natural History, vol. 27 (1920), p. 269; E. H. Morris, *The Temple of the Warriors at Chichen Itza, Yucatan: Description of the Temple of the Warriors and the Edifices Related Thereto*, Publication of the Carnegie Institution of Washington, vol. 1, no. 406 (1931), p. 100.
22. Pepper 1920, pp. 194–95, 375–76.
23. The illustrations of parallels from Mexico are admittedly selected at random. Similarities could be drawn from various Mexican groups and of varying horizons. The intention is to convey the idea that the elements are present in strength to the south.
24. Vaillant and Vaillant 1934, p. 121, fig. 27, a, b, (Gualupita III); S. Linné, *Archaeological Researches at Teotihuacan, Mexico*, Ethnographical Museum of Sweden, n.s. no. 1 (1934), pp. 184–86 (late period at Teotihuacan).
25. Cohabitation.
26. Ear plugs presumably of this type occur on figurines much earlier in the Hohokam culture, but actual specimens do not appear until the Sedentary period.

27. Gladwin, Haury, Sayles, and Gladwin 1937, pp. 130–34; Morris 1931, pp. 181–87.
28. Kelly 1938, fig. *27*, b (Chametla); Ekholm 1942, fig. *20*, h (Guasave); F. H. Scantling, "Excavations at the Jackrabbit Ruin, Papago Indian Reservation, Arizona" (Master's thesis, University of Arizona, 1940), pl. *16*, a–c (Jackrabbit Ruin).
29. E. W. Haury, "The Canyon Creek and Off Dwellings of the Sierra Ancha," Medallion Papers, no. 14 (1934), pp. 95–98; also from Ventana Cave.
30. In Central America a variation of this technique is seen in the textiles from the cenote at Chichen Itza (Peabody Museum collections). In the Hohokam layer of Ventana Cave, weft-wrap openwork was strongly represented; for occurrences among the Anasazi, see Haury 1934, p. 95.
31. Gladwin, Haury, Sayles, and Gladwin 1937, plates *77, 78*.
32. A similar situation has been deduced for northwestern Mexico (I. T. Kelly, "West Mexico and the Hohokam," *Tercera Reunión de Mesa Redonda Sobre Problemas Antropológicos de México y Centro América* [Mexico City, 1943], p. 216).
33. E. W. Haury, "Report of Ventana Cave" (in progress); see also E. W. Haury, "A Possible Cochise-Mogollon-Hohokam Sequence," *Proceedings of American Philosophical Society*, vol. 86 (1943).
34. Kelly 1938, p. 2; Kelly 1943, p. 216; Ekholm 1942, pp. 133–36.
35. Beals 1932, May 4, p. 159.
36. E. Anderson and H. C. Cutler, "Races of Zea Mays: I. Their Recognition and Classification," *Annals of the Missouri Botanical Garden* 29 (1942): pp. 84–85.
37. The Ventana Cave specimens were examined by Dr. Anderson who pronounced them not different from modern Pima-Papago corn in all essential characters as ascertainable from cobs.
38. Anderson and Cutler 1942, p. 84.
39. So far there is no good evidence of the kind of corn grown by them although the fact that they had corn at an early time (by the fourth century A.D.) seems fairly well established from the Arizona State Museum's findings in the Bluff site, Forestdale Valley (ten miles south of Showlow, Arizona).
40. This is strongly supported by recent work in the Bluff site, a village ascribable to the Mogollon people, with tree-ring dates in the early 300s (A. E. Douglass, "Checking the Date of Bluff Ruin, Forestdale: A Study in Technique," *Tree Ring Bulletin* 9 [1942]: 2–7).

    In addition to meager amounts of indigenous pottery, there were a few Hohokam intrusive sherds but none of Basketmaker origin, although Basketmaker pottery occurs in later horizons of the local chronology.
41. G. C. Vaillant, *Aztecs of Mexico* (Garden City, N.Y., 1941), pp. 26, 27.
42. Gladwin 1937, pp. 238–42. In Ventana Cave, where there was an

opportunity to examine the transition from prepottery, to pottery, no trace of the figurine complex in clay or in any other material was found in the prepottery debris.

43. Two have been found in the Bluff site, and while they are very simple, they are reminiscent of some Hohokam types.

44. S. J. Guernsey, "Explorations in Northeastern Arizona: Report on the Archaeological Fieldwork of 1920–1923," Papers of the Peabody Museum of American Archaeology and Ethnology, Harvard University, vol. 12 (1931), pp. 86–87.

45. Eckholm 1942, p. 134.

46. Very common in Classic period sites in both River and Desert Hohokam (particularly in the latter). While these are often red-slipped and polished, they seldom carry a design beyond simple incising. There are specific shape analogies to the simpler types at Chametla and Guasave (Kelly 1938, fig. *24*, a–i; Ekholm 1942, fig. *17*, a, q).

47. I find no actual reference to these from northwestern Mexico nor is there clear-cut evidence for them in Papagueria. They occur in greatest abundance in the River Hohokam (E. W. Haury, "The Excavations of Los Muertos and Neighboring Ruins in the Salt River Valley, Southern Arizona," Papers of the Peabody Museum of American Archaeology and Ethnology, Harvard University, vol. 24 (1945), pp. 109–11) and are dated to the Classic period. A southern origin for this trait is, frankly, an assumption, based on certain premises which cannot be recounted here.

48. G. F. Ekholm, "The Archaeology of Northern and Western Mexico," in *The Maya and Their Neighbors* (New York, 1940), pp. 325–26; Ekholm 1942, p. 77; A. M. Withers, "Excavations at Valshni Village, Papago Indian Reservation, Arizona" (Master's thesis, University of Arizona, 1941), p. 52.

49. D. D. Brand, "The Distribution of Pottery Types in Northwest Mexico," *American Anthropologist* 37 (1935): 300.

50. Withers 1941, pp. 36–43; also in Ventana Cave and other sites of the Arizona State Museum survey. The Trincheras sherds reported from Snaketown in Pioneer period context (Gladwin, Haury, Sayles, Gladwin 1937, p. 218) may not be interpreted as a case of fictitious association.

51. The Boquillas site of Sauer and Brand 1931, p. 93.

52. A. L. Kroeber, "Conclusions: the Present Status of Americanistic Problems," in *The Maya and Their Neighbors* (New York, 1940), p. 480.

53. Gladwin, in Sayles 1936, p. 94. The essence of the discussion here takes exception to Mr. Gladwin's statement, however, that the "earliest pottery-making culture of Chihuahua was derived from a source in southern New Mexico of Mogollon affiliation," and would refer this back to a southern Mexican source on the level of the Middle Cultures.

54. A. V. Kidder, "The Pottery of the Casas Grandes District, Chihuahua," in *Holmes Anniversary Volume* (Washington, 1916), p. 267.

55. Sayles 1936, p. 85.
56. Ekholm 1940, p. 329.
57. Beals 1943, pp. 191–99.
58. Ekholm 1942, p. 136.

**PART 9**

**Introduction**

1. William Duncan Strong, "An Analysis of Southwestern Society," in *The Classic Southwest*, ed. Basil C. Hedrick, J. Charles Kelley, Carroll L. Riley (Carbondale, Ill., 1973), pp. 110–54. This article first appeared in the *American Anthropologist*, n.s. 29 (1927): 1–61.

**13  Native Culture of the Southwest**

1. N. C. Nelson, "Chronology of the Tano Ruins," *American Anthropologist*, n.s. 18 (1916): 159–80. A. V. Kidder and S. J. Guernsey, *Archaeological Exploration in Northeast Arizona*, Bureau of American Ethnology, Bulletin no. 65 (1919). A nonstratigraphic attack on the sequential problem was made by Kidder in *Pottery of the Pajarito Plateau, Memoirs of the American Anthropological Association*, no. 2 (1915), pp. 407–62.
2. A. L. Kidder, *An Introduction to the Study of Southwestern Archaeology* (New Haven, 1924).
3. W. D. Strong, "An Analysis of Southwestern Society," *American Anthropologist* 29 (1927): pp. 1–61.
4. L. Spier's "Havasupai Ethnography," Anthropological Papers of the American Museum of Natural History, vol. 29 (1928), pp. 81–392, has appeared since the above was written.
5. H. K. Haeberlin, *The Idea of Fertilization in the Culture of the Pueblo Indians, Memoirs of the American Anthropological Association* 3 (1916): 1–55, 14, 17 ff.
6. C. Wissler, *The American Indian*, 2d ed. (New York, 1922), p. 219, map fig. *58.*
7. A. L. Kroeber, *Anthropology* (New York, 1923), p. 337, map fig. *34.*
8. C. Wissler, *The Relation of Nature to Man in Aboriginal America* (New York, 1926), p. 213.
9. The terminology is that advocated by the archaeological conference held at Pecos, August 1927, namely: Basketmaker I, hypothetical, non-agricultural; BM II, the classic BM with maize; BM III, "post-Basketmaker"; Pueblo I, "pre-Pueblo"; P II, early or small ruin Pueblo; P III, Great period; P IV, late prehistoric, including period of discovery; P V, after Spanish settlement or the Pueblo rebellion. See A. V. Kidder, "Southwestern Archaeological Conference," *Science* 66 (1927): 489–91.
10. F. H. Cushing, "Preliminary Notes on the Origin, Working Hypothesis and Preliminary Researches of the Hemenway Southwestern Archaeo-

logical Expedition," *International Congress of Americanists, Berlin, 1888* 7 (1890): 151–94.

11. Kidder 1924, p. 112.
12. C. Lumholtz, *New Trails in Mexico* (New York, 1912), p. 170.
13. W. J. McGee, *The Seri Indians*, Annual Report of the Bureau of American Ethnology vol. 17 (1898), pp. 9–296. See pp. 173–75, 182–85, pls. *32, 33*, figs. *17, 18, 39*.
14. Kidder 1924, p. 127, fig. *25*. Page 113 seems to suggest early P IV.
15. E. F. Schmidt, "A Stratigraphic Study in the Gila-Salt Region," *Proceedings of National Academy of Science* 13 (1927): 291–98.
16. Strong 1927, p. 49.
17. Ibid., pp. 52, 53, chart 2.
18. E. Seler, "Die alten Bewohner der Landschaft Michuacan," *Gesammelte Abhandlungen* 3 (1908): 133 (Tarascan); A. L. Kroeber, "*Handbook of the Indians of California,*" Bureau of American Ethnology Bulletin no. 78 (1925), p. 764 (Mohave: Chuhuecha, Satukhota tales); C. G. DuBois, "The Story of Chaup: A Myth of the Diegueños," *Journal of American Folklore* 17 (1904): 217–42 (Diegueño).
19. E. H. Morris, "The Beginnings of Pottery Making in the San Juan Area," Anthropological Papers of the American Museum of Natural History, vol. 28 (1927), pp. 125–98.
20. A. L. Kroeber, *Serian, Tequistlatecan, and Hokan*, University of California Publications in American Archaeology and Ethnology, vol. 11 (1915), pp. 279–90. Brinton made the first identification.
21. Series of islands lead from both the Peninsula and Angel de la Guarda island to Tiburon with intervals of open water probably nowhere exceeding a dozen miles in width—not an impossible distance to transverse in a balsa such as the Seri use in crossing back and forth between Tiburon and the mainland.
22. Edwin M. Loeb, *Pomo Folkways*, University of California Publications in American Archaeology and Ethnology, vol. 19 (1926), pp. 147–405), see p. 399.
23. Field information of J. H. Steward and M. R. Harrington.
24. Kroeber 1925, p. 900.
25. Ibid., p. 559.
26. Ibid., pls. *63, 72, 81*; E. W. Gifford and W. E. Schenck, *Archaeology of the Southern San Joaquin Valley, California*, University of California Publications in American Archaeology and Ethnology, vol. 23 (1926), pp. 41, 49–52, 99–109, pls. *1–13*.
27. Llewellyn L. Loud and M. R. Harrington, *The Lovelock Cave*, University of California Publications in American Archaeology and Ethnology, vol. 25 (1931).
28. Now on record in M. R. Harrington, *Tracing the Pueblo Boundary in Nevada*, Museum of the American Indian, Heye Foundation, Indian Notes, vol. 5 (1928), pp. 235–40.

29. Strong 1927; also William Duncan Strong, *Aboriginal Society in Southern California*, University of California Publications in American Archaeology and Ethnology (in press).
30. E. W. Gifford, "Miwok Lineages and the Political Unit in Aboriginal California," *American Anthropologist*, n.s. 28 (1926): 389–401.
31. A. E. Douglass, "Dating our Prehistoric Ruins," *Natural History* 21 (1921): 27–30; A. E. Douglass, "Some Aspects of the Use of the Annual Rings of Trees in Climatic Study," *Scientific Monthly* 15 (1922): 5–22; also oral communication to Pecos conference, 1927.
32. Wissler 1922, pp. 237, 238, 265, 266; R. Linton, "North American Maize Culture," *American Anthropologist* 26 (1924): 345–49; J. R. Swanton, "Southern Contacts of the Indians North of the Gulf of Mexico," *International Congress of Americanists, Rio de Janeiro, 1922* 20 (1924): 53–59; P. Rivet, "L'orfèvrerie précolombienne des Antilles," *Journal de Société des Américanistes de Paris*, n.s. 15 (1923): 183–213; W. H. Holmes, "Carribbean Influence in the Prehistoric Art of the Southern States," *American Anthropologist*, o.s. 7 (1894): 71–79. Since the above was written, C. D. Gower has reviewed the whole subject in *The Northern and Southern Affiliations of Antillean Culture, Memoirs of the American Anthropological Association*, no. 35 (1927).
33. C. Wissler, *The American Indian* (New York, 1917); Wissler 1922.
34. A. L. Kroeber, *The Tribes of the Pacific Coast of North America, International Congress of Americanists, Washington, 1915* 19 (1917): 385–401; A. L. Kroeber, "American Culture and the Northwest Coast," *American Anthropologist*, n.s. 25 (1923): 1–20.
35. Kroeber 1925, p. 916.
36. Wissler 1922, pp. 363, 374.
37. Ibid., p. 257.
38. Kroeber 1923.
39. Wissler 1922; Linton 1924; Swanton 1924; Rivet 1923; Holmes 1894; Gower 1927. In general the authors are conservative as to Antillean influence.
40. Swanton 1924, in a general discussion of the relations of the Southeast, leans toward transmission from Mexico via the Southwest, on the basis not so much of direct evidence as by inferred insufficiency of other routes. Linton, "Origin of the Skidi Pawnee Sacrifice to the Morning Star," *American Anthropologist*, n.s. 28 (1926): 457–66, posits two centers of origin in Mexico, probably coastal and highland, from which diffusions reached respectively the Southeast and Southwest, the Pawnee ceremony being the result of a blending of the two influences analogous to a blending which occurred among the Aztecs just before the Conquest.
41. M. R. Harrington, "The Ozark Bluff-Dwellers," *American Anthropologist*, n.s. 26 (1924): 1–21. On p. 14 he lists eleven Southwestern resemblances and eight pointing to the Southeast or other eastern areas.

42. W. H. Holmes, *Aboriginal Pottery of the Eastern United States*, Annual Report of the Bureau of American Ethnology 20 (1903), p. 67.
43. A. C. Parker, *The Archaeological History of New York*, New York State Museum Bulletin nos. 235–38 (1922), p. 1–743.
44. Warren King Moorehead, *Stone Ornaments, Used by Indians in the United States and Canada* (Andover, 1917), p. 257.
45. Wissler 1922, p. 218–20; Wissler 1926, pp. 80–95.
46. Rivet, 1923.
47. C. G. DuBois, *The Religion of the Luiseño Indians of Southern California*, University of California Publications in American Archaeology and Ethnology, vol. 8 (1908), pp. 169–86.

**PART 10**

**Introduction**

1. See, for instance, Elsie C. Parsons, "Spanish Elements in the Kachina Cult of the Pueblos," *International Congress of Americanists* 23 (1928): 588–89, 596.
2. Carroll L. Riley, "Mexican Indians in the Sixteenth Century Southwestern U.S.A.," *América Indígena* (in press).
3. Thomas Holien and Robert B. Pickering, "Analogues in a Chalchihuites Culture Sacrificial Burial to Late Mesoamerican Ceremonialism" (Paper presented at the 1973 meetings of the Society for American Archaeology).
4. Phil C. Weigand, Garmon Harbottle, and Edward V. Sayre, "Trade Patterns for Turquoise in Mesoamerica and Southwestern United States" (Paper presented at the 1973 meetings of the Society for American Archaeology.)
5. J. Charles Kelley, "Mesoamerica and the Southwest United States," in *Handbook of Middle American Indians* (1966), 2: 95–110.
6. Charles C. DiPeso, "Casas Grandes and the Gran Chichimeca," *El Palacio* 74 (1968): 45–61.

**14  Some Aztec and Pueblo Parallels**

1. Bernardino de Sahagún, *A History of Ancient Mexico*, vol. 1, trans. Fanny R. Bandelier (Nashville, Tenn., 1932).
2. E. C. Parsons, "Spanish Elements in the Kachina Cult of the Pueblos," *International Congress of Americanists* 23 (1928): 588–89, 596.
3. Sahagún 1932, p. 95. Again in the ceremony of the seventeenth month *all* the priests impersonate the gods, wearing masks. The priest impersonating the distinctive goddess of the ceremony wore a mask with two faces, one in the back and one in the front, the mouths very large and the eyes protruding (Sahagún 1932, p. 136). Pertinent in this connection and to the whole question of the development of the Pueblo mask cult is the

distinction at Zuñi between the priest's mask and the dancer's mask. "The Zuñi distinguish two types of masked impersonations, the katcinas, which I have called the dancing katcinas, and the katcina priests. The katcina priests do not come to dance. They never dance outdoors. If they dance at all it is before special groups, and in the kivas to the songs of other choirs. This is not considered dancing in the same sense as the dancing of the Kokokci or other groups who provide their own music. They come to perform certain priestly functions, to 'make the New Year,' to reaffirm the gods and bring their blessings, to initiate the children into the mysteries of the katcina cult. They are, indeed, priests wearing masks. They wear ancient masks, permanently associated with a single impersonation, which are tribal and not individual property. The impersonators are chosen either by the council or priests or by special cult groups who are the trustees of their ritual" (R. L. Bunzel, *Zuñi Katcinas*, Annual Report of the Bureau of American Ethnology, vol. 47 [1929–30*a*], p. 879).

The Kachina priest mask is presumably the pre-Conquest, Aztec-like impersonation, the Kachina dancer mask being the impersonation which has experienced more directly the Spanish influence, in particular the burlesque Kachina masks, Hewahewa of Zuñi, Gowawaima of Santo Domingo [see Leslie A. White, *The Pueblo of Santo Domingo, New Mexico, Memoirs of the American Anthropological Society*, no. 43 (1935), pp. 114–20].

4. Archaeological evidence for pre-Spanish use of the mask has just come to light through Dr. E. W. Haury who has studied in the Peabody Museum of Cambridge the collection made in 1887 or 1888 by F. H. Cushing from a ritual cave near Phoenix, Arizona. A ritual stick, perhaps a prayer stick, perhaps a Kachina "doll" or "baby," has painted on it an indubitable Kachina mask, parti-colored, with the characteristic Kachina doll ears. A bandolier is painted on the nude body. The stick suggests the encradled "baby" used by the Keres and associated with cave shrines (Noël Dumarest, *Notes on Cochiti, New Mexico, Memoirs of the American Anthropological Association* 6 [1920]: 141–42, fig. *3*). Haury believes the Arizona cave collection is Pueblo of the thirteenth or fourteenth century.

5. Diego Pérez de Luxán, *Journal, Expedition into New Mexico made by Antonio de Espéjo, 1582–1583*, trans. George P. Hammond and Agapito Rey (Los Angeles, 1929), p. 79.

6. E. C. Parsons, *Hopi and Zuñi Ceremonialism, Memoirs of the American Anthropological Association*, no. 39 (1933), p. 13. See Bunzel 1929–30*a*, pp. 1009, 1083–84.

7. Sahagún 1932, p. 45.

8. Parsons 1933, p. 13.

9. Sahagún 1932, p. 35.

10. He fails to state, for example, who function as curers for the mountain-sent or Tlaloc diseases. Presumably the Tlaloc priests do.
11. Sahagún 1932, p. 27.
12. E. C. Parsons, "Curanderos in Oaxaca, Mexico," *Scientific Monthly* 32 (1931): 60–61.
13. E. C. Parsons, Field notes on Cora and Huichol.
14. Wenima is a place of beautiful mountains, of pine and trees of all kinds, of lakes and meadows. Here are two kivas where the Shiwanna guard their flashes of lightning. Dumarest 1920, p. 173.
15. Sahagún 1932, p. 193. Inferably all these diseases proceed from the rain or water spirits—from lightning, water serpent, mountain rain spirits (gout being identified with rheumatism).
16. Dumarest 1920, p. 174; E. C. Parsons, "Notes on Ceremonialism at Laguna," Papers of the American Museum of Natural History, vol. 19, pt. 4, (1920), n. 2.
17. Cf. E. C. Parsons, *The Social Organization of the Tewa of New Mexico, Memoirs of the American Anthropological Association,* no. 36 (1929), p. 131.
18. Blue green is associated with lightning by the Zapoteca, as it is associated with the Kachina by the Pueblo.
19. E. C. Parsons, *Tewa Tales, Memoirs of the American Folklore Society* 19 (1926a): 194–95, 214–217.
20. E. C. Parsons, "The Origin Myth of Zuñi," *Journal of American Folklore* 36 (1923): 161. Note too that in Zuñi myth the Kachina were children who drowned in crossing a river.
21. Ralph L. Beals, Ethnology of the Mayo-Yaqui Indians.
22. E. C. Parsons, *Mitla; Town of the Souls and Other Zapoteca-speaking Pueblos of Oaxaca, Mexico* (Chicago, 1936).
23. Dumarest 1920, p. 209, fn. 2; E. C. Parsons, *Isleta, New Mexico,* Annual Report of the Bureau of American Ethnology vol. 47 (1932a), pp. 366–67; Parsons 1926a, p. 103.
24. We recall that the tradition of the drowned children occurs among Pima and Papago. E. C. Parsons, "Notes on the Pima," *American Anthropologist* 30 (1926b): 463; personal communication from Dr. Ruth Underhill. When I speculate about the sacrifice of turkeys or of turkey feathers by various Mexican and New Mexican peoples as analogous to human sacrifice, I recall the Hopi tale of the old couple who were not drowned in the flood but were changed into turkeys (Parsons 1923, p. 161n2). Bird sacrifice should not be overlooked among our parallels. The Aztec sacrifice quail; the Hopi, eagles. Possibly the Pueblo offering of turkey feathers (to the dead and the Kachina) has been a substitute for such turkey sacrifice as is general in southern Mexico and in Guatemala. Note that the Zuñi scalp-chief deposits wing feathers of the male turkey with the food he offers to a slain Navaho. His apostrophe to the

turkey cock (R. L. Bunzel, *Zuñi Ritual Poetry*, Annual Report of the Bureau of American Ethnology vol. 47 [1929–1930*b*], p. 677), indicates that the wing feathers represent the whole bird.

The Hopi, like the Aztec, ate dog, and Stephen reports one instance of a dog's head being offered with other food sacrifices to the Hopi god of death and fire. The dog was killed by the clowns who not uncommonly kill dogs, "play" which once may have had a sacrificial character. The Hopi dog Kachina indicates a belief in spirit dogs, as does also the existence on First Mesa of a dog "house" or shrine.

25. Dumarest 1920, p. 215.
26. At Zuñi one function of the scalps is divination.

> *He has become one to foretell*
> *How the world will be*
> *How the days will be.*
>
> [Bunzel 1929–30*b*, p. 680]

27. Sahagún practically states that for them a future life was expected. When the women to be sacrificed burned their clothing, jewels, chests, spindles, and weaving sticks it was said "that all these (jewels) would be given back to them in the other world after their death" (p. 126). Captives were actually adoptive in the warrior's family (Sahagún 1932, p. 77).
28. However, Pueblo lore about the children who drown and become Kachina and the lore about the mountain-dwelling spirit who captures children to devour come to mind. These bogey or monster masks among the Hopi, the Matashka, Fewkes has compared with coyote impersonations among the Aztec (J. Walter Fewkes, "On Certain Personages Who Appear in a Tusayan Ceremony," *American Anthropologist* 7 (1894): 32–52.

Possibly the offerings at Isleta and Taos to the stillborn or the child dead point to an early practice of child sacrifice. Isletans used to hide their children in covered jars or in the house walls against the arrival of the mountain giant who came into town with the mountain rain spirit, and it is said that the bones of children are to be found near the cave in the western mesa where the bogey lives.

29. Sahagún 1932, pp. 55, 126.
30. Parsons 1926*a*, pp. 184, 226, 231, 232, 277.
31. A. M. Stephen, *Hopi Journal*, Columbia University Contributions to Anthropology, (New York, 1934).
32. E. C. Parsons, "Zuñi Tales," *Journal of American Folklore* 43 (1930): 11, 43; F. Boas, *Keresan Texts*, Publication of the American Ethnological Society, vol. 8, pts. 1 and 2 (1928 and 1925).
33. Parsons 1920, p. 122.
34. Sahagún 1932, p. 126. Food is put into the mouth of the corpse by old women, among the Aztec. At Isleta two women feed the scalps (Parsons 1932*a*, pp. 257–58).

35. Sahagún 1932, pp. 148–49.
36. Ibid., pp. 52, 74, 75.
37. Ibid, p. 123.
38. It is characteristic of the ancient Tlaxcalans (F. Starr, "Notes upon the Ethnography of Southern Mexico," *Proceedings of the Davenport Academy of Natural Sciences* 8 [1899–1900]: 117), and Tarascans (F. Starr, *The Little Pottery Objects of Lake Chapala, Mexico*, Department of Anthropology Bulletin, University of Chicago, vol. 2 [1897]), and of the Zapotecas among whom to this day it survives. Sahagún describes (p. 134) miniature plates, boxes, and gourd cups for tiny offerings of food and drink to the mountain or rain spirits whose shrines were at the edge of the water. Here is a clue to the presence of the Tarascan miniatures in the waters of Lake Chapala.
39. Sahagún 1932, p. 81; Stephen 1934.
40. I use the term in the familiar sense, but, as we have been suggesting, it is far from certain that this expresses the Indian attitude; and see below.
41. Or almost lacking. In the prayers of the Zuñi scalp ceremony the blood of the enemy is referred to as "adding to the flesh of our earth mother" (Bunzel 1929–30*b*, pp. 680, 687).
42. Sahagún 1932, pp. 35, 36, 53, 64.
43. Ibid., p. 148.
44. Ibid., p. 35; E. C. Parsons, *The Pueblo of Jemez*, Department of Archaeology, Phillip's Academy (1925), p. 123; Bunzel 1929–30*a*, p. 845.
45. It is quite apparent that Sahagún had no conception of exorcism, of ritual to overcome supernatural danger, or the bad effects of broken taboo. All such rites he calls penance or punishment. It is quite possible that ritual bloodletting was an exorcising rite rather than a penitential rite. (Note Sahagún 1932, p. 131). Compare it with flagellation, which in Franciscan terms is penance, but in Indian terms is exorcism.
46. Sahagún 1932, p. 118.
47. Ibid., p. 96.
48. Ibid., pp. 158, 244.
49. Ibid., p. 41.
50. Ibid., pp. 151, 159. At Zuñi, the blood of a deer is smeared on the mouth of the mountain lion fetish. I know of no other Pueblo instance.
51. Ibid., p. 114.
52. Ibid., p. 40.
53. Among the eastern Pueblo miniature costumes are offered to the sun, and very small, if not miniature, water jars are used in the rain cult. I find no suggestion of the motif of the inexhaustible or of "much from little" in Sahagún, but in Zapoteca folk tales it occurs in just the same mode as in Pueblo folktales.

   The miniature prayer-image of what is wanted is another parallel between the Zapoteca and Pueblos.

54. Sahagún 1932, pp. 39, 70; Parsons 1925, p. 122.
55. Sahagún 1932, p. 157.
56. Ibid., p. 82.
57. Ibid., pp. 40, 41. See p. 623.
58. Ibid., p. 90.
59. Ibid., p. 25.
60. Ibid., pp. 44, 126.
61. Ibid., p. 27. Witches are seen (Pueblo) or see themselves (also a stone knife) (Aztec) in a bowl of water.
62. Ibid., p. 73.
63. Compare the clay corn kernel encrusted image of the horned water-serpent on the winter solstice altar of the Tewa of First Mesa with the dough image of the Aztec god which is given teeth of pumpkin seeds and eyes of black beans (Ibid., p. 46); and compare the tradition of the eastern Tewa that originally the image of the god of the Kossa was of dough. The prototypes of the Ne'wekwe of Zuñi and the Kashare of the Keres were of human cuticle or of the Earth of Corn Mother, i.e. of cornmeal. Bread in the shape of jackrabbits and turtles is given to the Isletan clowns by their aunts.
64. Ibid., p. 61; Stephen 1934; Parsons 1920, p. 118, fig. *19.*
65. Sahagún 1932, pp. 32–33. Here is a suggestion of why Catholic confession did not "take" among the Pueblo. (Only at Isleta is there any suggestion of acculturation between Catholic and Indian confessional practices). Formally, there may have been an opening; but psychologically there was nothing in common. See E. C. Parsons, "Further Notes on Isleta," *American Anthropologist* 23 (1921): 149.
66. Sahagún 1932, p. 191.
67. Ibid., p. 41.
68. Ibid., p. 197.
69. E. C. Parsons, "The Canes," *Mexican Folk-Ways* 7 (1932*b*): 81–86.
70. Sahagún 1932, p. 124.
71. Ibid., p. 97.
72. Ibid., p. 26.
73. Ibid., p. 97.
74. Stephen 1934.
75. Sahagún 1932, p. 120.
76. Ibid., p. 123.
77. Ibid., pp. 65, 138.
78. Ibid., p. 66.
79. Ibid., p. 81.
80. Stephen 1934. Note too that the Hopi place seed corn on the altar for a blessing. Cf. Sahagún 1932, p. 54.
81. Sahagún 1932, pp. 80, 92–93.
82. Stephen 1934.

83. Sahagún 1932, pp. 111–12.
84. Ibid., pp. 56, 93–94, 148.
85. Parsons 1932a, pp. 322–33.
86. Parsons 1920, p. 126.
87. Sahagún 1932, pp. 124–25.
88. Ibid., p. 107.
89. Ibid., p. 147.
90. Stephen 1934.
91. Ibid.
92. Sahagún 1932, p. 96. This burlesque or clowning in connection with human sacrifice suggests interesting speculation about early functions of Pueblo clowns. Their contemporary policing function hardly accounts for the dread they inspire. Besides, they are priests of the gods of water, the gods to whom human sacrifices would have been made by the Pueblo, if made at all.

 Note, in this connection, that at the Taos deer dance the Black Eyes give bits of raw venison to the "corn" dancers.
93. Sahagún 1932, p. 150.
94. Stephen 1934.
95. Sahagún 1932, p. 146.
96. Ibid., p. 132.
97. Leslie A.White, *The Acoma Indians*, Annual Report of the Bureau of American Ethnology, vol. 47 (1929–30), pp. 88–94.
98. Stephen 1934.
99. Elsie Clews Parsons, *Winter and Summer Dance Series in Zuñi in 1918*, University of California Publication in American Archaeology and Ethnology, vol. 17 (1918), p. 197; cf. Sahagún 1932, p. 176.
100. Sahagún 1932, p. 60.
101. Stephen 1934.
102. Sahagún 1932, pp. 60–61. There is a hint here of the nagual belief which survives among the Zapoteca and other peoples of Oaxaca. At the birth, ashes are strewn around the house at night and tracks are looked for to determine the animal (possibly also the lightning) familiar or guardian spirit.
103. E. C. Parsons, *Notes on Zuñi, Pt. I, Memoirs of the American Anthropological Association* 4 (1917): 188–89.
104. Sahagún 1932, p. 90.
105. Ibid., p. 69.
106. Bunzel 1929–30a, p. 962; see also pp. 846–47.
107. Four is also favored by the Aztec. Possibly the mixed culture of the Aztec is indicated in their uses of four and five.
108. Sahagún 1932, p. 147.
109. Ibid., pp. 27, 53, 82, 97.

110. H. R. Voth, *The Oraibi Powamu Ceremony*, Field Columbian Museum Publications, no. 61 (1901), pp. 98–99.
111. Sahagún 1932, pp. 173, 176.
112. Ibid., p. 173; O. LaFarge II and B. Byers, *The Year Bearer's People*, Middle American Research Series, Pub. 3, (New Orleans, 1931), pp. 113–14 (Nutla and other Zapoteca-speaking peoples).
113. Stephen 1934; Parsons 1920, p. 101.
114. Sahagún 1932, p. 202.
115. Stephen 1934.
116. Sahagún 1932, p. 197.
117. See A. F. Bandelier, "Report of an Archaeological Tour in Mexico," Papers of the Archaeological Institute of America, American Series, no. 2 (1884), p. 154.
118. Bunzel 1929–30a, p. 679.
119. Sahagún 1932, p. 242.
120. Ibid., p. 242.
121. Ibid., p. 70.
122. Ibid., pp. 133, 230.
123. Ibid., p. 194.
124. White 1935, pp. 114–20.

# INDEX

Acaxee, 59
Acoma, 47, 77, 122, 140, 144
Acus (A-qo), 43, 44, 45, 47
Africa, 7, 116
Aguascalientes, 54
Aguico, 47
Ahacus (Aguascobi), 44, 47
Ahuatuyba, 29
Alarcón, 6
Algonkins, 122, 123
All Souls Day, 139
Altamirano, 13
Anasazi, 4, 90, 94, 95, 96, 104, 130, 160
Antelope mesa, 77, 156
Antilles, 40, 118, 120, 124, 164
Apaches, 32, 33, 34, 35, 107, 125, 154
Aparico, Fray, 34, 35
Arapaho, 123
Archaic, 111, 117
Arid North America, 53, 58–59, 62, 156
Arikara, 122
Arizpe, 24
Arlegui, Fray Francisco de, 35
Arroyo del Nombre de Dios, 33
Arroyo de los Pilares, 33
Arroyo de San Diego, 32
Asa, 76
Ascension, 26, 27
Asunción, Fray Juan de la, 38, 41

Athabascans, 108
Augustan, 145
Awatovi, 61, 76, 77, 82, 83, 85, 86, 87, 156, 157, 158
Ayala phase, 10
Aztec, 6, 7, 12, 13, 50, 58, 62, 67, 117, 118, 128–46, 156, 166, 167, 168, 170, 171
Aztec ruin, 117

Babiácora, 154
Bacadéhuachi, 33
Bacuachi, 44, 154
Baja California, 40, 109, 111
Bamochi, 153
Bamori, 153
Baserac, 29
Basin, 53, 107, 112, 113, 118, 121, 123, 124
Bernalillo, 27
Bernardino, Father, 133
Blackfoot, 123
Bluff-dweller, 121
Bluff site, 160, 161
Brew, J. O., 4, 61, 66, 67, 130
Buena Vista Lake, 112
Bulitikibi, 83
Burrus, Father Ernest J., 24, 38

Cabeza de Vaca, 6, 41, 48
Caborca, 153
Caddoans, 123

Cáhita, 11, 50, 55, 56, 59, 60, 61, 62
Cahvilla, 113
Canaan, 116
Canyon de Chelly, 78
Caquima, 48, 155
Carretas, 34
Carrizo, 47
Casa Grande, 11, 15, 16, 22, 25, 46, 110, 157
Casas Grandes, 4, 10, 24, 25–36, 67, 90, 130
Casas Grandes, Valley of, 35
Casas Grandes River, 27, 30, 32
Castañeda, 154
Catholicism, 5, 156, 170
Caucasian, 123, 124, 125, 126
Cedros, 14, 151
Central America, 17, 21, 22, 60, 92, 116, 160
Cerillos, 130
Cerro de Montezuma, 31
Chaco Canyon, 4
Chalchihuites, 10, 116, 129, 130
Chametla, 161
Cherokee, 122, 124
Cheyenne, 123
Chichen Itza, 160
Chiva-no-ki, 46
Chumash, 125
Cibola, 43, 44, 45, 46, 47, 48, 154
Civano, 46
Civonaroco, 46
Coahuila, 54, 151
Cochise culture, 93, 97, 159
Cochiti, 26
Codex Mendoza, 151
Colorado of the West, 40
Colorado Plateau, 95
Colorado River, 6, 39, 41, 47, 82, 97, 108, 110, 112, 113
Colorado River tribes, 108
Colorado State, 29, 69, 76
Columbia-Frazier, 118

Cora, 50, 52, 56, 57, 59, 62, 100, 133
Coronado, Francisco Vásquez, 6, 7, 38, 45, 47, 48, 129, 153, 154, 155
Corralitos, 26
Crook, Gen. George, 32
Crow, 123, 124
Cuicuilco, 98
Culiacán, 7, 42, 46, 154
Cushing, Frank Hamilton, 27, 38, 46, 47, 70, 74, 106, 108, 155, 166

Datura, 114
Deming, N. M., 25
Desert culture, 90, 104
Díaz, Melchior, 6, 155
Durango, 10, 12, 54, 99, 129

El Paso, 34, 35
El Paso del Norte, 34, 35
Espejo, Antonio de, 46, 47, 140
Esteban (Steven), ix, 6, 38, 41, 42, 43, 44, 45, 48, 155, 168
Eudeves, 42, 153

Fewkes, J. Walter, 74
First Mesa, 142, 168, 170
Flagstaff, 15
Folsom, 94
Forestdale Valley, 160
Fort Huachuca, 24
Fort Thomas, 46
Franciscans, 34, 41, 42, 45
Fresnal, Arizona, 109

Gabrielino, 125
Galeana, 25
Gatlin, 4
Gila culture, 104, 109, 110, 119
Gila Pueblo, 15, 17, 93
Gila River, 6, 25, 39, 41, 46, 99, 108, 109, 157
Globe, Arizona, 15
Gros Ventre, 123
Gualterio Abajo, 10

Guanajuato, 54
Guasave, 67, 130, 161
Guatemala, 41
Guaymas, 43, 153
Gulf Coast, 124, 151
Gulf of California, 13, 94, 111
Gulf of Mexico, 6, 29, 121
Guzmán, Nuño de, 7, 40

Hacu (Hacus, Ha-cu-quin), 47
Hano, 76, 81, 84, 86–87, 157
Havasupai, 107
Hawikuh (Havico, Ha-vi-cu), 47,
    155
Hidatsa, 122, 123, 124
Hohokam, 4, 11, 15, 16, 18, 22, 52,
    60, 70, 90, 93, 94, 95, 96, 97, 98,
    100, 101, 104, 129, 160, 161
Hokan, 62
Honani, 79
Hopi, 68, 69, 74, 75–87, 115, 121,
    128, 131, 132, 134, 136, 137, 138,
    139, 140, 141, 142, 143, 144, 145,
    146, 156, 157, 167, 170
Huachinera, 25, 29
Huasteca, 52
Hue-hueri Kita, 25
Huichol, 50, 52, 56, 57, 62, 100, 116,
    133

Ibarra, 24
Iroquois, 122, 124
Isla del Angel de la Guardia, 153
Isleta, 133, 134, 138, 139, 146, 168,
    170
Isopete, 6
Ixtapalapan, 134

Jalisco, 10, 11, 52, 100
Janos, 16, 27, 34, 35
Jeddito, 67, 68
Jemez, 26, 27, 87
Jesuits, 13, 33, 34
Jocomes, 34–35

Kansas, 6
Kawaika, 77
Keres, 75, 76, 86, 132, 136, 145, 156,
    157, 166, 170
Keresan, 77, 87, 134, 135, 140, 143
Kino, 153
Kokop, 87
Koyemshi, 138

Ladder Trail, 78
Laguna, 135, 139
Lake Chapala, 169
La Playa, 100
La Quemada, 116
La Venta, 50, 62
Lincoln, 136
Little Colorado, 69, 80, 81, 82, 85
Los Muertos, 161
Lower California, 54
Luiseño, 125
Lumholtz, Charles, 57, 109
Luxán, 132

Macaqui, 48
Mandan, 122, 123
Marata, 43, 44, 45, 47
Marcos de Niza, ix, 6, 38, 39, 40–48,
    153, 155
Maricopa, 104, 107
Martyr, Peter, 13
Maski Skeleton House, 77
Matamoras, 151
Matape, 42, 43, 153, 154
Ma-tya-ta, 47
Matzaki, 48
Maya, 10, 15, 116, 117, 142, 156
Mayo, 134
Mayo River, 40, 101
Mazapil, 14
Mendieta, Fray Gerónimo, 39
Mendoza, Don Antonio de, 41, 45,
    155
Mesa Central, 52
Mesa Verde, 74

Mexico City, 47, 66, 134
Middle America, 17, 60, 61, 97, 119, 125
Middle Formative, 50
Mimbres, 70, 96, 100
Mississippian culture, 7, 123
Mississippi River, 121, 122
Missouri River, 123
Mixtecas, 133
Mocorito River, 52
Mogollon, 94, 95, 96, 97, 98, 100, 101, 130, 160, 161
Mohave, 104, 108, 109, 112
Montezuma, 34, 35
Moqui, 29, 46, 47
Morgan, Lewis H., 24
Motolinía, Fray Toribio, 39
Muskogi, 124
Mututicachi, 154

Nacori, 153
Nadal, Fray Pedro, 38, 41
Nahua, 117
Nahuatl, 6, 34, 129, 134, 141
Natchez, 121, 124
Navaho, 78, 84, 104, 107, 115, 125, 167
Nayarit, 10, 11, 52, 100
Negrete, 13
Nevada, 53, 54, 107, 112, 113
Niman, 138, 142
North America, 15, 21, 40, 50, 55, 92, 115, 116, 156
Northwest Coast, 104, 118, 119, 120
Nuevo León, 54, 55

Oaxaca, 151, 158, 171
Obregón, 24
Old Shumopavi, 86
Oñate, 8, 76
Onorato, 42
Opata, 6, 25, 33, 34, 43, 44, 45, 46, 47, 50, 62, 153, 154
Oraibe, 75, 78, 156, 157

Otermin, Governor, 35
Otomi, 117
Owakülti, 75, 80

Padilla, Juan de, 7, 39
Paiute, 121
Palanganas, 26
Paleo-Indian, 90
Palo Duro Canyon, 6
Pánuco, 7
Papago, 8, 56, 60, 61, 97, 104, 107, 125, 160, 167
Papagueria, 99, 100
Patayan, 94
Pawnee, 124, 164
Peabody Museum, 166
Pecos, 2, 6, 7, 69, 158
Pecos Chronology, 104
Phoenix, 11, 70, 166
Pima, 6, 8, 25, 29, 38, 41, 43, 44, 46, 50, 56, 60, 61, 87, 97, 104, 107, 109, 153, 154, 157, 160, 167
Piros, 27
Plains, 6, 104, 119, 121, 122, 123, 124
Plateau, 97, 118, 119, 123, 124
Platte River, 123
Plumed Serpent, 87
Pochteca, 7, 67
Pomo, 111
Pueblo Bonito, 27, 95, 117
Puerto de San Diego, 32
Puyé, 33

Queres, 26, 27, 33
Quetzalcoatl, 137
Quito, 41
Quivira, 6, 7

Rio de Palanganas, 31
Rio de Piedras Verdes, 31
Rio des Casas Grandes, 26
Rio Grande, 26, 27, 69, 76, 77, 79, 80, 83, 84, 86, 87, 121

Rio Puerco, 69
Rio Soto de la Marina, 52
Rodrigo, Fray Antonio de Ciudad, 42

Salado, 100
Saltillo, 12
Salt River, 6, 87
Salt River Valley, 14, 18, 76, 161
San Antonio, Church of, 35
San Buenaventura, 32, 35
San Dieguito, 93, 94
San Felipe, 26
San Ildefonso, 26, 139
San Joaquin Valley, 112
San Juan, 69, 76, 84, 108, 131
San Luis Potosí, 12
San Mateo, 28
San Miguel de Culiacán, 42
San Pedro River, 44, 46, 99, 154
Santa Ana, 26, 27
Santa Barbara, 112
Santa Clara, 33
Santa Fe, New Mexico, 4, 35, 130
Santo Domingo, 146, 166
Schroeder site, 10
Seri, 43, 109, 111, 153, 163
Shoshoneans, 114
Showlow, 160
Shumopavi, 77
Sichomovi, 75, 76, 78, 85, 87
Sierra de la Madera de Casas Grandes, 32
Sikyatki, 67, 68, 77, 81, 82, 83, 86, 87, 157
Sinaloa, 40, 41, 42, 52, 54, 55, 67, 97, 99, 130
Sinaloa River, 63
Siouans, 123
Snaketown, 4, 11, 15, 17, 93, 161
Sobaypuris, 44, 45, 47
Sonoran Desert, 12
Sonora River, 43, 101

Sonora Valley, 6, 24, 154
Sumas, 34, 35
Supai, 82

Tamaulipas, 54, 121
Tanoan, 62, 132
Taos, 121, 131, 136, 138, 139, 144, 145, 168, 171
Tarahumares, 33, 62, 116, 125
Tarascan, 5, 6, 7, 60, 100, 117, 169
Tcewadi, 87
Tehachapi, 112
Tehuas, 26, 33
Teotihuacan, 5, 62, 117
Teotleco, 129, 141
Tepehuan, 50, 56, 62
Tewa, 75, 76, 77, 78, 79, 80, 81, 83, 84, 86, 87, 145, 156, 170
Tiburon island, 111, 153, 163
Tiguas, 27, 132
Tlaloc, 58, 61, 67, 70, 128, 130, 131, 132, 167
Tlalocan, 133
Tlaxcalans, 169
Toltec, 4, 6, 40, 116, 117, 118
Toltec, Arizona, 17
Torquemada, Augustín, 13
Totonac, 117
Totonteac, 43, 45, 46, 47, 155
Trincheras culture, 99, 100, 101, 161
Tuba, Arizona, 82
Tucson, 25
Tula, 4, 62
The Turk, 6, 7
Tusayan, 47

Uto-Aztekan, 56, 62

Vacapa, 42, 43, 44, 153
Vatican, 28, 38
Ventana Cave, 94, 97, 160, 161
Verde, 69
Viejo, San José del Pueblo, 46

Walapai, 107
Walpi, 76, 77, 79, 85, 86, 157
Willow Spring, 82

Yaqui drainage, 24
Yaquis, 13, 42, 46, 59, 125, 134
Yavapai, 107
Yokuts, 112
Yumans, 55, 56, 59, 61, 97, 107,
    108, 110, 111

Zacatecas, 12, 54, 129, 151

Zapoteca, 117, 133, 134, 139, 167,
    169, 171
Zàrate-Salmeron, Fray Geronimo
    de, 47
Zea maize, 61, 97
Zia, 26, 27
Zippe, 135
Zuñi, 6, 29, 38, 46, 47, 48, 59, 77,
    78, 79, 80, 81, 85, 87, 106, 122,
    128, 129, 131, 132, 133, 134, 135,
    136, 137, 138, 139, 140, 141,
    142, 143, 144, 145, 146, 154, 155,
    156, 157, 166, 167, 169, 170